Palgrave Studies in Ethics and Public Policy

Series Editor: **Thom Brooks,** University of Durham, UK

Palgrave Studies in Ethics and Public Policy is a series publishing research monographs and edited books. The series delivers cutting edge work on issues of contemporary interest explored from across a broad range of disciplinary and methodological approaches. These books will provide leading contributions in the area of ethics and public policy shaping debates. They are aimed at a broad readership from academics and their students to policymakers.

Titles include:

Thom Brooks (*editor*)
ETHICAL CITIZENSHIP
British Idealism and the Politics of Recognition

Chris Chapple
THE MORAL RESPONSIBILITIES OF COMPANIES

Nir Eisikovits
A THEORY OF TRUCES

Nolen Gertz
THE PHILOSOPHY OF WAR AND EXILE

Annamari Vitikainen
THE LIMITS OF LIBERAL MULTICULTURALISM

Palgrave Studies in Ethics and Public Policy
Series Standing Order ISBN 978-1-137-28168-5 (hardback)
                        978-1-137-28169-2 (paperback)
(*outside North America only*)

You can receive future titles in this series as they are published by placing a standing order. Please contact your bookseller or, in case of difficulty, write to us at the address below with your name and address, the title of the series and one of the ISBNs quoted above.

Customer Services Department, Macmillan Distribution Ltd, Houndmills, Basingstoke, Hampshire RG21 6XS, England

An Expressive Theory of Punishment

Bill Wringe
Bilkent University, Ankara, Turkey

First published 2016 by
PALGRAVE MACMILLAN

Palgrave Macmillan in the UK is an imprint of Macmillan Publishers Limited, registered in England, company number 785998, of Houndmills, Basingstoke, Hampshire RG21 6XS.

Palgrave Macmillan in the US is a division of St Martin's Press LLC, 175 Fifth Avenue, New York, NY 10010.

Palgrave Macmillan is the global academic imprint of the above companies and has companies and representatives throughout the world.

Palgrave® and Macmillan® are registered trademarks in the United States, the United Kingdom, Europe and other countries.

ISBN: 978–1–137–35711–3

This book is printed on paper suitable for recycling and made from fully managed and sustained forest sources. Logging, pulping and manufacturing processes are expected to conform to the environmental regulations of the country of origin.

A catalogue record for this book is available from the British Library.

A catalog record for this book is available from the Library of Congress.

For Charlotte and Max: heaven knows what they will make of it.

Contents

Acknowledgments

Several chapters in this book draw on, and reproduce either in part or in whole, work which has previously appeared in print. I am grateful to Springer for permission to reproduce material from the following articles: 'Must Punishment Be Intended to Cause Suffering?' *Ethical Theory and Moral Practice* 16 (4) pp. 863–77 (which forms the basis of Chapter 2); 'Perp Walks and Punishment' *Ethical Theory and Moral Practice* 18 (3) pp. 615–29 (which forms the basis of Chapter 5); 'War Crimes and Expressive Theories of Punishment: Communication or Denunciation?' *Res Publica* 16 pp. 119–33 and 'Why Punish War Crimes? Victor's Justice and Expressive Justifications of Punishment' *Law and Philosophy* 25 (2) pp. 159–91, parts of which appear in Chapter 6. I am also grateful to Wiley Blackwell for permission to reprint material from 'Collective Agents and Communicative Theories of Punishment' *Journal of Social Philosophy* 43 (4) pp. 436–56, which forms the basis of Chapter 7.

I would like to thank each of the following for encouragement and support, whether intellectual, practical or emotional, and in many cases for penetrating comments on one or more draft chapters, or on papers which contributed to this book: Varol Akman, Istvan Aranyosi, John Baker, Sally Barclay, Radu Bogdan, Chris Bennett, Sandrine Berges, Max Berges, Sandy Berkovski, Thomas Besch, David Copp, Helen Brown Coverdale, Janet Brennan Croft, Liz Disley, Antony Duff, Rob Fisher, John France, Max de Gaynesford, Margaret Gilbert, Shane Glackin, Joshua Glasgow, Nathan Hanna, Gaye Heathcote, İrem Kurtsal Steen, Fragano Ledgister, Ambrose Lee, Kourken Michaelian, Monica Mookherjee, Adam Morton, Mark Nelson, Andrei Poama, Diana Richards, Lucas Thorpe, Lars Vinx, William von Bulow, Simon Wigley, Jack Woods, Ally Wringe, Charlotte Wringe, Colin Wringe.

While I was writing or, too often, not writing this book, the commentariat at Making Light provided me with entertaining and enlightening conversation on too many occasions to recall, and I would like to thank them both individually and collectively, as well as Teresa Nielsen Hayden and Patrick Nielsen Hayden for bringing the blog and the conversations it supports into existence, and also Avram Grumer, Abi Sutherland, Jim MacDonald and Idumea Arbacoochee for moderating and sustaining it. My greatest debt is, of course, to Sandrine Berges, without whom nothing would have been either started or finished.

Part I
The Paradigmatic Case

1

Punishment: Some Questions Philosophers Ask

1 Punishment – everyday understanding and philosophical theory

Most of us – that is to say, most adult members of developed societies – would probably claim to have some idea of what punishment is. We might make good on this claim by being able to identify a few paradigmatic instances of punishment; by showing that we can distinguish things which are punishment from things which are not but which might, superficially, appear somewhat like it; or by giving a rudimentary account of the sorts of roles which punishment appears to play in our own societies. Understanding what punishment is, in this fairly minimal sense, need not involve having a philosophically adequate definition of punishment. It also need not involve anything that deserves the title of a philosophical *theory* of punishment. Still, one might wonder why one should need anything more than this fairly minimal understanding of punishment.

Here is one answer. The minimal understanding of punishment which I have just outlined falls short of answering all the questions that a reflective person might raise when thinking about the role of punishment in our lives. For example, it need not include any account of why we punish – of the goals which we take the institutions of punishment to serve. This seems a pity. States invest considerable resources in punishing individuals, and there is often public debate about what forms of punishment should be administered to which individuals. If we do not know what we are trying to achieve when we punish people, we are in a poor position to assess whether the means we are taking to those ends are effective – or appropriate.

The minimal understanding of punishment which I have just described also leaves us without answers to questions about whether the sorts of measures we take in punishing people are justified. We can distinguish between a number of questions that someone might raise in this area. First, we might ask whether the goals which we pursue in punishing people are worthwhile goals. In doing so, we would be asking whether these are goals that we should be pursuing at all. Secondly, we might be asking about whether the means we adopt are appropriate to these ends: whether they are likely to be effective at all; whether they conflict with other goals that we might have; whether other means to the same ends might not be justifiable; and so on.

Finally we might ask whether the means we adopt in pursuing the goals we have in punishing people are permissible. Philosophical discussions of punishment often start from the observation that punishment typically involves treating people in ways which we would not take to be justifiable in contexts other than that of punishment. It often involves imprisoning them – depriving them of their liberty; or imposing monetary fines, depriving them of part of their property. In some places it may even involve killing them, by ritual means. It is less often remarked upon, but no less true, that punishment has in the past involved treating people in ways which many of us would not now take to be justifiable in any context whatsoever. So we should not necessarily assume that the forms of treatment that we now describe as punishment are ones which can be guaranteed to be justified simply because of the context in which they now occur.

I have argued that there are many questions about punishment which might be raised by a reflective person and which are not necessarily answered by our pre-reflective understanding of the nature of punishment. I have also suggested that many of these questions depend on our understanding of the goals of punishment. But it might not be obvious why we need a *philosophical* account of punishment in order to answer them, rather than say, a sociological account, or a historical one, or a jurisprudential one. Indeed, it might seem as though these other disciplines are more likely to be able to tell us about the goals of punishment than philosophy is.

In order to answer this question, I need to say something about the nature of philosophy and its relationship to other disciplines. I shall not attempt to give a definition of philosophy, since I take it to be an intellectual discipline consisting of a loosely related family of inquiries, each with its own history, self-understanding, and conception of its relationship to its past. Instead I shall try to focus on three features which I take to be characteristic of philosophical inquiry.

First, philosophy explicitly aims at generality. One might think that this is a feature of any kind of inquiry, insofar as any kind of inquiry makes use of a conceptual repertoire, and the purpose of concepts is to classify things in terms of features that they share. But this is not necessarily true. It has sometimes been thought to be characteristic of the human sciences that they aim at understanding particulars in their particularity. Thus one might aim to understand the penal code of a particular society, or its operation at one particular time and place, without any presumption that other penal codes in other places and in other societies have operated in the same kinds of way. Indeed, one might do so with the particular aim of illustrating the ways in which different societies understand their activities.[1]

Secondly, philosophers – or at least philosophers in the analytic tradition with which I identify myself – often take themselves to be interested, at least in part, in conceptual questions. Thus we are, at least in part, concerned with whether there is something fundamental to the way in which we think about punishment that explains why certain kinds of action constitute acts of punishment rather than acts of private or publicly sanctioned revenge or taxes on an unpopular or socially disadvantageous activity; and if so what it takes for something to be correctly classified as punishment rather than as an instance of one of these other kinds of activity.

The fact that philosophy is partly concerned with conceptual questions is closely connected with the fact that it aims at generality. If there is anything to be learnt about punishment by considering our concepts, this would go some way towards explaining how it is possible for us to acquire understanding at the level of generality which I have suggested that philosophy aims at, by the kinds of means which philosophers typically employ. It would be natural to think that if it is possible to acquire an understanding of punishment which delivers insights at

---

[1] Someone might object that in doing so one was aiming at bringing about a general understanding of the fact that different societies vary in their particularity; but it would be unusual for a historian, say, to explicitly identify this as their aim. In any case, since we are not trying to arrive at a set of necessary and sufficient conditions for something's being a work of philosophy, this should not bother us too much: we might want to say that someone who worked with this kind of aim was trying to arrive at a kind of philosophical understanding via the medium of history.

a great level of generality, this is only likely to be possible on the basis of a very wide-ranging knowledge of how punitive institutions have worked in different times and places. However, although philosophers may illustrate their views by reference to a wide range of examples, few of them have thought wide-ranging knowledge of different penal institutions and penal systems is a prerequisite for giving a philosophical account of punishment; and even fewer have possessed it.

If we can acquire knowledge about punishment by reflection on conceptual matters, this presents a less serious problem than one might think. This is not to say that a knowledge of features of different kinds of penal system, or to the history of such systems, is irrelevant to the kind of understanding which a philosophical account of punishment aims at providing. For I have not claimed – and shall not be claiming – that philosophical inquiry is exclusively concerned with conceptual matters. (We shall see at least one reason why this is so in a moment.) However, it does suggest ways in which some of the issues with which philosophers are concerned when they discuss punishment might be prior to or independent of historical, sociological or jurisprudential inquiries about punishment. This is because they concern whether we should take the deliverances of those inquiries to be concerned with punishment rather than with something else.

We might think there is a problem with the idea that we might rely on a philosophical account of punishment rather than a historical or sociological one to tell us what punishment really is. Compare what I have said about the relationship between philosophical accounts of punishment and other kinds of account of the phenomenon to the relationship that we might take to exist between philosophy and the physical or biological sciences. We would not expect philosophers of physics or biology to be in the business of elaborating philosophical accounts of life or of matter, and relying on those accounts to tell us whether biologists and physicists were talking about life and matter. Why should philosophers who are interested in the nature of punishment stand in a different relationship to their subject matter than philosophers who are interested in the nature of life or of matter?

The answer to this question is relatively straightforward. First, we should notice that a philosopher might well be interested in providing a detailed philosophical elaboration of our everyday conception of matter or of life. Having done so, they might well point out ways in which this conception differs from that which is embodied in one scientific discipline or other. However, we would not normally expect a physicist or biologist to be especially bothered by being told this: given their purposes our everyday conceptions of life or of matter are likely to be irrelevant to them.

Someone writing about punishment in a jurisprudential or socio-logical vein might take the same attitude. There need not be anything problematic about doing so. Still, there are questions to which people investigating punishment in these ways might take their work to be relevant that are not simply questions which belong to one particular scientific discipline. The sorts of questions which I have in mind here are questions about legitimation – that is to say, questions about which sorts of social practice can be justified. Since answers to questions about legitimation are – at least in societies like our own, addressed at least in part to ordinary citizens and not just to fellow academic specialists – they need to be answered in ways which either draw on a widely accepted understanding of punishment or which make clear the ways in which the conceptual framework on which the intellectual endeavors of the specialist depend differ from the concepts which are in the repertoire of the ordinary citizen.[2]

So far I have argued that there are questions about the nature of punishment which we are unlikely to be able to answer satisfactorily without a philosophical account of punishment. I have also argued that one thing that is likely to be characteristic of a philosophical account of punishment is that it should involve some kind of reflection on concep-tual matters. However, I stopped short of claiming that a philosophical account of punishment would be a purely conceptual one. One reason why I did so should now be fairly clear. I have argued that the questions about punishment to which a philosophical account of punishment might be relevant include some that concern the legitimacy or justifi-ability of certain social institutions. Questions of this sort are, of course, normative questions; and normative questions are ones which philoso-phers interested in punishment have typically aimed to shed light on.

This is the third of the three features which I described as being char-acteristic of philosophical enquiry: its concern with normative issues. In making this claim about what is characteristic of philosophical enquiry I am not claiming that all philosophical issues are normative ones. Clearly, they are not. Nevertheless, philosophers qua philosophers typically take normative questions to fall within the boundaries of their discipline in a way that practitioners of other disciplines do not.

---

[2] The same is also true when the scientist stops addressing an audience which is made up only of scientists and addresses matters of public policy, concerning themselves with, say, questions about risk or disaster prevention.

This third characteristic feature of philosophical enquiry is distinct from, though related to the previous two. It is connected to the concern with generality, insofar as philosophers will typically be concerned with the justifiability of certain general features of an institution such as punishment, and not whether its operations are justified in one or other particular case. Its connection with philosophy's concern with conceptual matters is slightly more subtle. Some philosophers have thought that normative questions could be resolved simply by reflecting on the nature of our concepts.[3] However, very few philosophers who are now writing would accept this view. So although a philosophical account of punishment will address conceptual questions, it will address other kinds of question as well. We should expect reflection on conceptual matters to shed light on questions of justification, (and perhaps to rule out some candidates for answering them) but we should not expect it to settle them on its own.

2 Some philosophical questions about punishment, and their motivation

I have suggested that there are a number of questions about punishment which might occur to a reflective individual, and which the minimal understanding of punishment which I described at the beginning of the first section would not help us to answer. I also argued that a philosophical account of punishment might play a role in helping us to answer these questions. However, I did not suggest that the questions which a philosophical account of punishment might help us to solve are in any way exclusively philosophical: indeed I argued that the reverse is true.

This is not to deny that there is a set of questions about punishment to which professional philosophers have paid particular attention. Clearly there are such questions, and we shall be looking at a range of them during the course of this book. However questions which a philosophical account of punishment might help us to answer need not be (and in my view are not) questions which only a philosopher would have reason to raise.

I have already suggested that accounts of what punishment is might be relevant to answering questions about the justification of punishment. I shall now expand on this point. It is sometimes suggested that there are particular difficulties in explaining how the institution of

---

[3] See for example Locke 1975 book 3 chapter 11 paragraph vi.

punishment might be justified. Those who think this typically have a certain conception of punishment in mind. On the account in question, something can only constitute punishment if it involves some kind of unpleasant or burdensome treatment inflicted on someone who is taken to have transgressed some kind of norm. Furthermore, not every kind of burdensome treatment inflicted on someone who is taken to have transgressed a norm will constitute a form of punishment. For something to be punishment, the harsh treatment must be inflicted on the person who has done wrong with the intention of placing a burden on them, and because of the transgression that they have committed.

It is natural to think that, when other things are equal, there is something wrong with intentionally inflicting hardship on another individual. One might go even further and claim that people have a right not to have such treatment inflicted on them in such circumstances. Finally, one might add that, whatever goals one might have in inflicting harsh treatment on another individual, one should, where possible, attempt to achieve these goals in ways which do *not* involve intentionally inflicting harm on others. One straightforward reply to this is that punishment involves a situation where other things are *not* equal, and that the fact that this is so and the reasons why it is so are sufficient to undermine the presumption against intentionally inflicting harm on others. Unfortunately, it is surprisingly difficult to provide a convincing account of precisely why this should be the case. One might be tempted to conclude from this – as some authors have – that because this is so, the institution of punishment is in fact *not* justified.

In this book I shall take a different approach. In responding to the case against the justifiability of punishment, I shall make three main claims. First, I shall argue that although it is no accident that punishment typically imposes hardship on those who are punished (and indeed that anything which did not have this feature would not constitute a form of punishment), it is nevertheless a mistake to suppose that punishment needs to involve the intentional inflicting of burdensome treatment on those who do wrong. I shall also argue that even if it is true that we have a right not to have burdensome treatment deliberately inflicted on us, it does not follow that we have a right not to suffer from the normal and foreseeable workings of our penal institutions. Finally, I shall argue that the goals of punishment are ones which cannot be achieved in ways which do not involve burdensome treatment being inflicted on individuals. So we cannot expect that societies find other ways of achieving these goals. (We can, of course ask whether these goals are worth achieving: I shall argue that they can be.)

If this line of argument is successful, I will have shown how some views about the justifiability of punishment depend on a particular conception of what punishment is. Still, one might naturally think that this falls short of showing that a philosophical account of punishment can help us to see how punitive institutions can be justified. To suppose otherwise would be to start off from the idea that the institutions of punishment have some kind of presumption in their favor, and showing them to be justified is simply a matter of undermining arguments which are intended to overturn this presumption.

There might be some social institutions which are so deeply embedded in the fabric of our lives that this is the only form which a justification of them could possibly take. For example, one might think that this is true of the institution of the family, understood in a fairly broad sense as essentially involving a small group of individuals, living on intimate terms with one another and having a particularly close concern with one another's interests.[4]

Could punishment be an institution of this sort? One might think so. However, I do not think that this is correct. It is certainly true that it is difficult for us to imagine a complex society which did not involve something analogous to the notion of punishment. But it may be that this simply involves a failure of imagination on our part. In any case, whether or not it is true that punishment, understood in its widest possible sense, is an ineliminable part of our lives, this is surely not true of the institution that is at the centre of most philosophical discussions of punishment – namely the institution of legal punishment, inflicted by a modern state. For it is far from obvious whether the contemporary state is the only form of social organization which is open to us.

If it is to be possible to give a justification of our existing institutions of punishment, then we need some kind of idea of the sorts of goals which we think those institutions can justifiably seek to achieve. Different accounts of the ways in which punishment by the state might be justified have given different accounts of what these goals are. Some have taken punishment to be a means of channeling individuals' natural retributive instincts in a way that prevents them from undermining social stability; others have taken it to be a way of deterring individuals

---

[4] It would not necessarily follow from a view like this that particular *forms* of family life – in particular, forms involving a particular conception of marriage, or of the essential roles of partners in a marriage, could be taken to be presumptively justified. For experience teaches us that these have varied in significant ways between different historical periods and in different cultures.

from committing crimes; others that of rehabilitating or reforming offenders, and so on. In this book, I shall be exploring and arguing for one particular view about the nature of punishment. At its centre is the idea that punishment is, in an important sense, a communicative act. It is a way in which a society can express collective condemnation of certain kinds of behavior. For reasons which will presumably be obvious, I shall call this the 'expressive conception' of punishment.

3   The expressive conception of punishment – some preliminaries

The idea that punishment has an expressive dimension is not uncommon. Given the views I have already expressed about the reasons why we might want a philosophical account of punishment, any philosophical account of punishment which had this character would be extremely unlikely to be correct. For I have argued that a plausible philosophical view of punishment must, to some extent, be immanent in our everyday understanding of what punishment is. And if this is true, it would be extremely surprising, to say the least, if aspects of it did not show up when intelligent people reflected on the nature of punishment.

In fact, aspects of the expressive view can be traced back to such historical figures as Hegel, Durkheim, and James Fitzjames Stephen.[5] Contemporary discussions of the view typically trace it back to Joel Feinberg's essay, 'The Expressive Function of Punishment'.[6] In that essay, Feinberg argued that in order for us to be able to distinguish clearly between acts which constituted genuine cases of punishment and other responses to behavior which a state might want to discourage, we need to recognize that it is an essential to an act's constituting punishment that it should express a form of social disapproval of a particular kind of action.

Feinberg's suggestion that punishment necessarily has an expressive function was intended as a contribution to the analysis of our concept of punishment rather than as part of an attempt to justify punitive institutions. However his insights have been appropriated by a number of theorists who have suggested, in different ways, that the fact that we need to pay proper attention to the expressive dimension of punishment

---

[5] Hegel 1942 (first published in 1821); Stephen 1967 (first published in 1873); Durkheim 1933 (first published in 1891).

[6] Feinberg 1965.

if we are to give an adequate account of how and why our punitive institutions can be justified.

There is something slightly ironic about this. As Anthony Ellis has noted, Feinberg thought that the existence of an expressive dimension to punishment made it harder rather than easier to justify punitive institutions.[7] But in some ways we should not find it especially surprising. If we hold that punishment is (or can be) justified, whereas non-punitive impositions of harsh treatment that are analogous to punishment would not be, then we are likely to be drawn towards a consideration of ways in which punishment differs from these other non-punitive forms of harsh treatment. And if Feinberg's claim that it is precisely the expressive dimension of punishment that makes the difference is correct, we should not be surprised to find this fact featuring in accounts of how punishment is justified.

Many expressive acts – though not all – are directed at an audience. If we accept that punishment has an expressive dimension it is natural to ask whether punishment is an expressive action of this sort or whether it is more appropriate to regard its expressive dimension as being analogous to, say, facial expressions of emotions. The fact that such expressions can occur when an individual has no reason to think that they are being observed suggests that they need not have an intended audience (although they might conceivably be explicable in terms of the effect that they standardly have on their audiences).

The idea that punishment might be a form of expressive behavior which does not have an intended audience seems, at least on the face of it, to be compatible with the idea that we need to appeal to the essentially expressive dimension of punishment to explain the difference between punishment and non-punitive forms of harsh treatment. However, there seems to be little beyond this to recommend it.[8] It is certainly hard to see how the fact that punishment was distinctive in this respect could contribute in any way to explaining how punishment could be justified; and to the best of my knowledge, no advocate of an expressive theory of punishment has adopted it.

So it is, perhaps, more likely to be fruitful to think of punishment as involving an attempt to express something to some audience. The question then arises of who this audience might be. On the face of it there seem to be three distinct possibilities here. One is that punishment is intended to communicate something to an offender; the second that it is supposed to communicate something to the community in which

---

[7] Ellis 2012.
[8] I shall consider it in more detail in Chapter 4.

both offender and victims are members. The third possibility is a hybrid of the first two: on an account of this sort, punishment is intended to communicate a message both to the offender and to society at large.

Antony Duff has defended an account of punishment of the first sort.[9] As we shall see in due course, he holds that the punishment involves harsh treatment imposed on an offender for a moral wrong which expresses a society's disapproval of a certain form of behavior, and which is aimed at inducing remorse and regret on the part of the offender. Duff's account involves a distinctive conception not only of punishment but also of the nature of criminal law and the role of the criminal trial in establishing guilt.[10]

Duff's account has many virtues: we shall consider some of them in due course. However, it is also worth saying something about its limitations. Duff takes as his paradigm case of punishment the imposition of sanctions on an individual by a community of which he is a member. The community need not be a state: although we typically think of states as being paradigmatic examples of political communities, at various points in his writing Duff considers examples other kinds of communities such as universities and religious communities. Nevertheless it seems as though for Duff's account to make sense, we must think of the relevant sorts of communities not simply as groups of individuals subject to a common set of rules but as groups in which membership in the community is something it makes sense for individuals to value. If we do not do so, it is difficult why we should think of the harsh treatment which punishment involves as being an occasion for repentance rather than simply resentment.

I shall not dispute the claim that many cases of punishment, including those which we are most likely to think of when we look for instances of justifiable punishment, fit this model very well. One might argue that there is something problematic about the idea of membership in a state being something which it makes sense for its members to value: perhaps there are many individuals in many states whose experience would suggest that this account of what the state offers them is too optimistic. But by the same token, these are individuals living in states whose legitimacy – and the legitimacy of whose institutions – is perhaps open to question.

More significantly, there seem to be many significant examples of kinds of punishment which we might be inclined to regard as being

---

[9] See in particular Duff 1986, 2001.
[10] See in particular Duff 2007.

legitimate but which do not seem to fit Duff's paradigm particularly well. One kind of case which is likely to occur to many people is the case of the punishment by a community of individuals who are not members of that community. States typically claim the right to punish not only their citizens but also non-citizens who commit crimes on their territory. We might try to subsume these under Duff's paradigm by thinking of individuals who enter the territory of a state which is not their own as being granted a kind of temporary membership of the state whose territory they occupy. However, it is less obvious that it makes sense to think of temporary membership in such a state as being something which the individual being punished has some reason to value – indeed, insofar as it opens him or her up to harsh treatment that would otherwise be illegitimate it may be appropriate to regard it as involving a burden rather than a benefit.

The case of the punishment of non-citizens may be regarded as being little more than a philosophical puzzle. Someone might hold that in an ideal world, individuals committing crimes on the territory of other states would simply be detained and handed over to the authorities of their own state. One problem with such an arrangement would be that different states have different laws, so that behavior which is criminal under the laws of one state might not be criminal under the laws of another state. Still, we can at least see how the account might be developed: perhaps states could be seen as imposing on their own members the duty to obey local law when in foreign countries, so that individuals who break the law when abroad become liable to punishment in their own states. (An account of this sort would explain why it was not only appropriate but desirable for individual who are being punished in a foreign country to be repatriated.)

However, this concern as to whether Duff's account can be adapted to cover cases where it does not seem plausible to regard the subjects of punishment as being members of a community that is imposing punishments is at the root of concerns about three more consequential kinds of case with which I shall be particularly closely concerned in this book. These are the punishment of individual war criminals, the punishment of domestic corporate crimes and the (putative) punishment of states for large-scale international crimes.

Much of this book will be concerned with articulating a version of the expressive conception which can say something illuminating about punishment, and about its justifiability in these kinds of cases. I shall argue that we have good reasons to want an account of punishment on which it makes sense to talk of punishment, rather than revenge or retaliation in such cases. Versions of the expressive account on which the principal audience of the communication which punishment involves is the offender are, I shall argue, unlikely to provide us with what we want. What we shall need in each case – or so I claim – is an account on which the punitive communication is addressed to a wider audience. I shall refer to accounts of this sort as 'denunciatory' versions of the expressive conception of punishment. My aim in this book is to show that an account of this sort can be justified.

Describing my account as a 'denunciatory' account risks one kind of misunderstanding that may be worth pre-empting at this early stage. I have introduced the account by contrasting it with Duff's 'communicative' account of punishment.[11] On that account the goal of penal communication is to evoke a certain emotional response in an offender – that of remorse or regret. One might assume there is a kind of symmetry between denunciatory and communicative accounts in this respect, with a denunciatory account being aimed at evoking a different kind of response in an offender: namely that of shame for wrongdoing. Many theorists have proposed accounts of punishment which have precisely this goal.[12] However, that is not the kind of account I am proposing. Three brief points should suffice to make the differences between my own position and that of those who advocate such accounts clear.

First, for many of the non-paradigmatic cases in which I am interested – in particular the cases of the punishment of collective entities, such as business corporations and states – the goal of shaming an offender seems entirely irrelevant. I shall not argue – though some might – that collective entities cannot undergo emotional states such as shame. It seems more significant that whatever positive role shame might have in helping individuals re-integrate into a community in the domestic case, there is little reason to suppose that collective shame might play a similar role in helping to restore collective entities which have offended against legal norms to a state where they might be less disposed to do so.

Second it is simply not clear whether accounts of punishment on which punishment aim at shaming offenders should be counted as denunciatory accounts at all, on my usage of the term. Such accounts seem to share with Duff's the idea that the goal of punishment is to induce, via communication, a certain kind of mental state in the offender. The idea

---

[11] I am grateful to my colleague Lars Vinx for comments which prompted this clarification.

[12] For useful discussion see Brooks 2008; Rodogno 2009.

seems to be that an offender will come to be ashamed by being aware that he or she is being shown, in public, to have a certain low status. If so, then although what is envisaged seems to involve a method of communication which is significantly more indirect than the one Duff envisages, it is nevertheless a form of communication with the offender (and, to draw on a distinction which will play a role in the argument of Chapter 3, with the offender qua offender, rather than with the offender qua member of a political community).

Third, and perhaps most importantly, along with many critics of shame-based punishments, I take the shaming of offenders to be a problematic cost of punishment rather than something that we might justifiably aim at. Indeed, this fact will play a significant role in my argument for the superiority of denunciatory accounts of paradigmatic instances of punishment over their communicative rivals: I shall argue that on the communicative account, our standard forms of punishment shame and stigmatize offenders in ways that the communicative account is unable to justify (whereas on the denunciatory account, such shaming and stigmatization as occurs seems inseparable from punishment's playing the expressive role which it does).

4   The road ahead

As may already be clear, some of the issues with which I shall be concerned in this book are ones which I take to have been neglected in many recent philosophical discussions of punishment. For this reason, it may be helpful to give a brief account of the main issues that I shall be addressing, the order which I shall be addressing them, and the ways in which they relate to the expressivist conception of punishment which is at the core of the book.

In the first half of the book, I shall be concerned with articulating a general account of legal punishment, focussing on the paradigmatic case of the punishment of an individual citizen for an offence against the laws of a political community of which he or she is a member. I shall start off, in Chapter 2, by arguing on more detail for the claim that we should adopt an expressive approach to punishment. In Chapters 3 and 4 I consider more carefully the form that the expressive account should take, paying particular attention to the question of what exactly we should take punishment to be expressing, who would take to be doing the expressing (Chapter 3), and who we should take the audience of the expression to be (Chapter 4). These three chapters will constitute the core of the first part of the book.

In the second half of the book, I shall attempt to apply this account to a number of 'non-paradigmatic' cases of punishment. In Chapter 5 I shall consider cases where an individual is punished, or might be taken to be punished, for an offense for which they have not yet been convicted (either because the offence has not yet been committed, or because no-one has yet been convicted). In Chapter 6 I shall consider the punishment of corporate agents by a state: here I will argue that denunciatory accounts are superior to communicative accounts. In Chapters 7 and 8, I move beyond the confines of the individual state to consider what my account can tell us about the punishment of individual war criminals and of states under both actual (in the case of individuals) and possible (in the case of states) international legal systems.

2

Punishment, Harsh Treatment and Suffering

1 Punishment and the intention to cause suffering

In Chapter 1, I introduced the idea that punishment might be seen as having a communicative function. However, I said very little about what might make that view attractive. My aim in this chapter is to do precisely that: I shall argue that there are good reasons for incorporating considerations about the expressive function of punishment. If we do so, we can avoid a problem which some recent authors have taken to stand in the way of any attempt to justify punishment. The problem arises from consideration of what appears to be a truism: when we punish people, we intend to make them suffer.

My aim here is somewhat limited. I am not attempting to provide anything that might claim to be an expressive justification of punishment. Although I think that expressive considerations play an important role in explaining how punishment can be justified, showing that they can do so will involve addressing a range of objections to the institution of punishment that I shall not be addressing here, and which it will not be worth considering until we have a more fully developed expressive account on the table. My aim is simply to address one significant objection to the practice of punishment, which is likely to have occurred to almost anyone who has considered punishment from a philosophical point of view, and which has played a central role in recent discussions.

Philosophical discussions of punishment often start with an attempt to give a general characterization or definition of punishment. One example is H.L.A. Hart's well-known account of punishment as involving harsh treatment, inflicted on an offender by an appropriate authority, in response to some specifiable form of wrongdoing.[1] David Boonin and Nathan Hanna have recently argued that this characterization of punishment either obscures or leaves out something important, namely that when we punish other people, we intend to make them suffer.[2] Boonin puts the point like this:

> Punishment involves *acting with the intention of harming someone* because she has (or is at least believed to have) committed an offense.[3]

Similarly, Hanna remarks that

> To punish an offender, one must aim to hurt or harm her in some way; the treatment to which she is subjected must be used at least in part as a way of making her suffer.[4]

Whether Hart's characterization leaves out or merely obscures the fact that punishment involves an intention to inflict suffering on an offender depends on how one understands the notion of harshness. If, like Hanna, we think that the best way of understanding the word 'harsh' in Hart's characterization of punishment is to say that it is treatment that aims to make someone suffer, then mentioning that when we punish someone we intend to make them suffer will simply be a matter of making salient something which that characterization leaves implicit.[5] I shall be suggesting, in the course of this chapter, that this is not the best way of understanding the notion of harshness.

Boonin and Hanna both think that the fact that punishment typically involves an intention to cause suffering presents a significant obstacle to anyone who thinks that the practice of punishing offenders can be justified. Hanna has argued, in a series of recent papers, that the fact that punishment constitutively involves an intention to cause suffering undermines a range of strategies for justifying punishment (including retributive strategies); while Boonin claims that reflection on this fact shows that punishment cannot be justified at all.[6]

---

[1] Hart 1959.
[2] Boonin 2008; Hanna, 2008, 2009a, b.
[3] Boonin 2008 p. 21 (italics mine).
[4] Hanna 2008 p. 126.
[5] Hanna 2012 pp. 124–8.
[6] Hanna 2008, 2009a, 2009b, 2014; Boonin pp. 12–17 and passim.

I shall be arguing that punishment need not involve an intention to cause suffering, and that attempts to show that punishment is unjustified which rely on this claim cannot be sustained. I shall draw on expressivist ideas in order to defend the claim that punishment need not involve an intention to cause suffering. If we take expressive goals of the right sort to form part of the definition of punishment, treatment can be characterized as harsh even if it is not intended to cause suffering.

My argument will not involve denying that punishment typically, foreseeably and predictably brings about suffering. Everything I say will concern the question of whether the narrower claim that punishment needs to involve an intention to cause suffering is true. One might think, then, that the issue being discussed is philosophical in the pejorative sense: a narrow matter, with no significant practical upshot. However, this is not true.

If punishment must involve an intention to cause suffering, attempts at punishment which do not make offenders suffer are failures. It might then seem appropriate to object to a punitive regime visited on some individual that it does not make them suffer (or that it does not make them suffer enough); or to attempt to assess the degree to which a convicted offender has actually suffered, and to supplement the punishment if they have not actually suffered, or not suffered enough. However, if punishment need not involve an intention to cause suffering, there is no reason to think this is appropriate.[7] So understanding whether or not punishment must involve an intention to cause suffering is something we might expect to have a significant impact on the way we treat convicted offenders.

2   The importance of intentions

It is widely acknowledged, and indeed, easy to see that punishing someone frequently involves harming them in various ways. We might think that this feature of punishment plays a significant role in explaining why punishment stands in need of justification at all. For, other things being equal, we might think that we should try to avoid harming people, at least when it is easy to do so. However, it is also fairly easy to see that the mere fact that punishment does sometimes harm other people is not enough to establish conclusively that punishment can never be justified. For it is highly implausible to suppose that we

---

[7] Of course there may be other ways of blocking the line of argument sketched here.

can never be justified in acting in ways that harm others. Sometimes we can be permitted to harm others in order to prevent significant harms to others and ourselves (as in cases of self-defense and the defense of others); and it seems intuitively plausible that on some occasions we are entitled to ignore knock-on effects of our actions in pursuing our own goals.

In Chapter 3 and 4 of this book, I shall be discussing how advocates of an expressive conception of punishment might respond to questions about the justifiability of punishment that arise from recognizing the fact that it causes harm to offenders. Boonin and Hanna's objection is slightly different: what they find problematic about punishment is precisely that it involves an *intention* to cause suffering, and not for example, that it does so reliably or foreseeably.

Neither Hanna nor Boonin think that the fact that a practice causes suffering, or even that it causes foreseeable suffering makes that practice impermissible in the same way that the intention to cause suffering does. For example, both hold that requiring criminals to pay restitution is legitimate even when this will harm the criminal, because it does not involve an intention to harm those individuals.[8] And Hanna suggests that one reason why both expressive and deterrent-based attempts to justify punishment fail is that there are ways of achieving the same expressive or deterrent-based ends as punishment does, but which do not involve an intention to cause suffering.[9] The existence of alternatives to punishment which do not involve an intention to cause suffering would only count against these justifications of punishment if there was something peculiarly objectionable about having an intention to cause suffering.

Neither Boonin nor Hanna say much in defense of the claim that there is something peculiarly objectionable about having the intention to cause other people to suffer. However it seems plausible that they are

---

[8] Boonin 2008 pp. 213–76; Hanna 2008 pp. 138–9.

[9] Thus for example Hanna 2008 pp. 127–8 writes: 'In what follows I will assume that the aim to impose suffering is essential to punishment, and will argue that this characteristic, in conjunction with other considerations undermines ER.' (ER is Hanna's abbreviation of 'Expressive Retributivism', his name for the version of expressivism he discusses.) The 'other considerations' that Hanna refers to are that there are ways of achieving the valuable goals which the expressive retributivist takes punishment to achieve and which do not involve an intention to cause suffering; and that there are moral reasons against doing something which is intended to cause suffering to another person in order to achieve a morally valuable goal if there are alternative ways of achieving this goal which avoid doing anything which is intended to cause suffering. For a similar point in the context of deterrence-based accounts, see Hanna 2014.

correct. There are many situations where we will judge someone who harms another person more harshly when we learn that they did so intentionally. Consider a trivial example. If you accidentally cause me to suffer by standing on my toe while wearing stiletto heels you are at worst careless, inconsiderate and clumsy. If you do it with intent to injure me, then other things being equal, that seems much worse. In saying this we need not be committed to the view it is always impermissible to have the intention to cause suffering: if you are treading on my toe because you think it is the only way to draw my attention to the fact I am about to knock you over with my heavy bag, this may well be permissible. However, the presence of feasible alternatives does seem to matter: if there are other ways in which you can alert me to the problem with my bag, then it is plausible that you should adopt them.

3   Defending punishment: an expressivist response

Boonin and Hanna seem to be right in thinking that there is something problematic about having an intention to cause suffering. However, it is unclear whether this really shows that punishment cannot be justified. We can see that something is amiss here by noting that their concerns appear to make little contact with the sorts of issues that typically motivate people who are concerned with penal reform. Their arguments for the unjustifiability of punishment do not commit us to very much by way of action to reform the institutional means by which we respond to criminal wrongdoing. For example, they do not show that there is something wrong with the practices of imprisoning people, imposing cripplingly large monetary fines upon them, or even executing them. They simply show that there is something wrong with doing this for the purpose of making people suffer.[10]

One natural response to this point would be to say that in practice, many of these ways of responding to wrongdoing involve an intention to impose suffering. This may well be true. Perhaps it is even true that we could not eliminate the intention to cause suffering from our penal practices without engaging in large-scale reform. Nevertheless, there seems to be something counter-intuitive about the idea that a society which executed, imprisoned, or fined people in response to criminal wrongdoing but which did so without making it part of its aim to make offenders suffer would be a society in which punishment had been abolished.

---

[10] For a more typical version of eliminativism about punishment see Golash 2005.

One attractive feature of expressivist views of punishment is that they help us to see why this is so. For, as I shall now argue, the expressivist position contains resources which enable us to argue that punishing someone need not necessarily involve an intention to make them suffer.[11] On an expressive theory of punishment, an important part of the justification of punishment consists in the messages it conveys. Some expressivists follow Joel Feinberg in taking the expressive dimension of punishment to be partially constitutive of something's being punishment.[12] For them, harsh treatment, which is a response to wrongdoing by an appropriate authority, should only be counted as punishment if it is intended to express a message of disapproval to those who perpetrate those crimes, or to society as a whole, or both. Other expressivists do not take the expressive dimension of a practice of responding to wrongdoing to be part of what makes it into punishment. However, authors of both sorts hold that, whether or not it is constitutive of something's being punishment, the expressive messages which punishment is intended to express play a significant role in justifying punishment.[13]

Different expressivists have different views about the role the expressive dimension of punishment plays in justifying punishment.[14] On Duff's 'communicative' view, punishment is a way in which a society can communicate its condemnation of wrongdoing to offenders in ways which prompts them to experience regret and remorse, both of which can play a valuable role in allowing them to be re-integrated into society.[15] For Christopher Bennett, punishment is a way in which society expresses certain 'reactive attitudes'. Punishment's justifiability derives from the

---

[11] Hanna 2008 and Boonin 2008 both take their arguments to be as effective against expressive conceptions of punishment as any others. But in doing so they both take the expressivist to be committed to a conception of punishment on which punishment must involve an intention to cause suffering. I aim to show that they need not be.

[12] Duff 2009; Feinberg 1965. Duff sometimes suggests that this is part of the definition of punishment, and sometimes that it is central to the justification of punishment, but not definitional. See for example Duff 2001 pp. xiv–x.

[13] As we shall see representatives of expressivism differ on many issues. Important contributions to the expressivist family include Duff 1986, 2001; Hampton 1992; Metz 2000, 2007; and Bennett 2008.

[14] One important way of classifying expressivist theories is by considering the intended audience of the message expressed. However, Joshua Glasgow (Glasgow forthcoming) has argued that the best form of expressivism is what he calls 'pure expressivism' on which punishment has no intended audience. I discuss this view in more detail in Chapter 4.

[15] Duff 2001.

right criminals have to be punished, which derives from their right to be treated as fully responsible members of their political communities, and to undergo a form of treatment which involves a form of symbolic penance.[16] Finally on a 'denunciatory' view of punishment, of the sort which I shall be defending in this book, the purpose of the harsh treatment that punishment involves is for a society to communicate to its members that certain norms are in force and that transgressions against them are viewed seriously.[17]

Expressivists often suppose that the state has a duty to communicate certain messages about certain kinds of wrongdoing either to the individuals who have acted wrongly (as on Duff's view) or to society as a whole (as on Metz's).[18] This point is not enough to justify imposing on offenders the sorts of treatment which we typically take punishment to involve: imprisonment, community service, monetary fines, and the like – forms of treatment often involve things which those subjected to them would rather not undergo. Call treatment of this sort 'burdensome treatment'. (On this definition, whether a form of treatment is burdensome depends on how those on whom it is inflicted respond to it, and not on the intentions of those who impose it. I may impose treatment which I know to be burdensome on someone with the intention of making them suffer. But I may also impose burdensome treatment without having this intention: for example, I may think that someone is so hardened, or so desperate, that a short stay in prison will do them no harm, but choose to impose it anyway. It may be that I am mistaken in this belief. If so, I will have imposed burdensome treatment without any intention to cause suffering.)

Different expressivists explain why we need burdensome treatment to achieve the communicative goals of punishment in various different ways. For example, Duff suggests that in punishing an individual, we are communicating something to him or her about the wrongness of his or her action in the hope that this will bring about repentance and remorse. Imposing burdensome treatment is a way of trying to make the wrongdoer focus on their wrongful action in a way which they might be less likely to do if the state communicated with them about the wrongfulness of their acts in some other way, such as receiving a condemnatory letter from a magistrate or other state official.[19] Bennett argues that the imposition of something burdensome is a way in which the state

---

[16] Bennett 2008.

[17] See also Metz 2000, 2007; Wringe 2006.

[18] Compare Metz 2000.

[19] Duff 2001 pp. 107–9.

can express a form of censure which is 'symbolically adequate' to the offense: because it does so, the offender is compelled, as Bennett puts it 'to undertake proportionate apologetic action as a way of undoing public wrong'. According to Bennett the censure must involve something burdensome, in order to be 'symbolically adequate': what the punished individual undergoes should be able to be understood by society at large as an appropriate and proportionate form of apology; and only burdensome treatment can be so understood.[20] Finally, on what I call the denunciatory view, which I shall defend at greater length in Chapters 3 and 4, the imposition of burdensome treatment is a way in which a punishing authority can express to a community that the infringement of certain kinds of norms is taken seriously – again, the suggestion is that purely symbolic, non-burdensome acts of condemnation could not do this as effectively.[21]

If an expressivist conception of punishment is correct, punishing someone need not involve an intention to cause suffering. Or so, at any rate, I shall claim. I shall argue that although punishment must involve harsh treatment, it does not follow from a form of treatment's being harsh that imposing it must involve the intentional imposition of suffering. Furthermore treatment which is harsh but which does not involve an intention to cause suffering can fulfill the expressive goals that expressivists take to play an essential role in justifying punishment.

4 Understanding harshness

Why do Hanna and Boonin hold that punishing someone must involve an intention to cause them to suffer? This claim seems to go beyond the characterization of punishment given in the first paragraph of this paper. On the face of it, that characterization makes no reference to such an intention: it only speaks of the treatment involved being 'harsh'. The same is true if we add to this minimal characterization the requirement, drawn from Feinberg, the expressivist claim that the harsh treatment be aimed at conveying a message of disapproval, either to the offender, or to society as a whole.

The minimal characterization does make some reference to intentions, since it says that something can only be punishment if it is a response to wrongdoing; and, plausibly, the phrase 'a response to wrongdoing' is best understood in a way which presupposes that something can only

---

[20] Bennett 2008 pp. 106–7.
[21] See also Wringe 2006 p. 180 for an earlier formulation.

constitute a response to wrongdoing if those who are inflicting it intend what they are doing as a response to wrongdoing. It is also implausible that harsh treatment inflicted on a wrongdoer *accidentally* constitutes punishment, even if it could be correctly described as a response to wrongdoing. Nevertheless, having an intention to respond to wrongdoing need not entail having an intention to cause suffering.

Hanna argues that something important is obscured by the fact that the characterization of punishment that I have given in the first paragraph makes no explicit reference to punishment's involving an intention to cause suffering. On his view, the notion of harsh treatment is best understood as treatment that it is intended to cause suffering.[22] I disagree: I shall argue that the right way of understanding the notion of harsh treatment which figures in the characterization of punishment given in the first paragraph of the paper is that it is treatment which would normally be found burdensome by a typical individual of the kind on whom it is being imposed. Notice that while it is true that, on an account of this sort, punishment need not involve an intention to cause suffering, it is nevertheless a non-accidental feature of punishment that it often does cause suffering. It is thus consistent with a claim Duff makes and Hanna highlights:

> Punishment aims to inflict something painful or burdensome on an offender...nor are this pain and this burden mere unintended side effects of a procedure which is not designed to be painful or burdensome.[23]

My case against Hanna does not turn on the verbal difference between something's being burdensome and something's causing suffering, but the difference between something's being actually intended to cause suffering to a particular individual and its merely being of a kind which is liable to cause suffering to individuals of that kind.

The existence of a difference is established by the following argument. If I inflict on you some treatment which is designed to cause you to suffer, and you do not in fact suffer, then I have to that extent failed. If my goal is important enough, it may be appropriate to inflict some other treatment on you. But if I intend to inflict on you some treatment which would typically cause suffering in individuals like you and you do not suffer, then I have not necessarily failed. I *may* have failed:

---

[22] Hanna 2008 pp. 124–7; 2009a p. 330.
[23] Duff 1992 p. 49; quoted by Hanna 2008 p. 127.

I may be mistaken about what individuals like you would find burdensome. Furthermore, if I have not made you suffer, this may be evidence that I am mistaken about exactly that. However, this evidence might be misleading. Perhaps I have failed because, very unusually, you have become a convinced Stoic while awaiting sentence, and now believe that imprisonment is not a way in which you can be harmed.[24] Or perhaps you have fallen into an uncharacteristic state of insensibility. In these cases, I have not necessarily failed in the goal of inflicting treatment that someone like you would normally find burdensome.

In arguing that this conception of harsh treatment is distinct from Hanna's, I am appealing to the principles that action types with distinct success conditions are distinct; and that success conditions are distinct if one can be fulfilled while the other is not. These principles are both general and plausible. So the characterization of harsh treatment offered here is distinct from Hanna's. On the other hand it is a characterization on which punishment typically will cause suffering, and on which the fact that it does so is non-accidental. In the normal course of events, not every individual on whom punishment is inflicted will be an atypical individual of their kind.

Admittedly, there is no logical bar to its being the case that every individual on whom punishment is inflicted should be an atypical individual of their kind. However, it is vanishingly unlikely that this will actually occur: it would require a kind of cosmic coincidence. It is not an important objection to an account of harshness that if such a cosmic coincidence were to occur, it would be untrue that harsh treatment typically caused suffering. For we have no need of a justification of punishment that would hold in such unusual cases. An account which shows punishment to be justified in worlds like the actual world, in which there are no cosmic coincidences of this sort, should be good enough for us.

One might object that although on my account punishing someone need not involve an intention to cause them to suffer, it involves something equally problematic: namely, the imposition of burdensome treatment on individuals simply because it is burdensome. Here, we need to make a distinction. We might understand 'burdensome' in a way in which it follows from the fact that I have imposed burdensome treatment on X that X has actually been burdened. On my account of

---

[24] Ancient Stoics like Epictetus held that 'the only way I can be harmed is to become less virtuous' (Epictetus 1928 *passim*). My argument does not require that the reader accept the Stoic view, but only that someone else might do so.

harshness, it does not follow from the fact that X has been punished that they have actually been burdened. So in this sense of 'burdensome', it is not true that on my account punishment imposes anything at all on people *because* it is burdensome. Punishment does not fail of its object if it fails to impose something which is burdensome in this sense.

Alternatively, we might understand 'burdensome' to mean 'that which many people might find to impose a burden'. If this is what 'burdensome' means, my account does entail that punishment involves the imposition of something burdensome because it is burdensome. However, it does not entail that that punishment involves the imposition of something burdensome because it is burdensome *and for no other reason*. Part of the point of the expressive account is that punishment involves the imposition of burdensome treatment because of the expressive goals that this is supposed to achieve. Furthermore, as I pointed out in Section 2, on some versions of expressivism, *only* burdensome treatment could achieve these goals.[25] (By contrast, it is not true that only treatment intended to cause suffering could achieve these goals.)

There might be something wrong with imposing burdensome treatment on people because it is burdensome and for no other reason. On my account, punishing someone does not do this. One might also think that there is something wrong with imposing burdensome treatment on people because it is burdensome in pursuit of some other worthwhile goal, and in particular in pursuit of a goal to which those on whom the treatment is may not consent. But neither Hanna nor Boonin commit themselves to anything so subtle: what they object to is the intentional inflicting of suffering.

Furthermore, we have already seen that Hanna and Boonin hold that although it is wrong to intentionally inflict suffering on other people, it is not wrong to inflict treatment on people which we can foresee would make them suffer, in order to achieve valuable goals to which they may not consent (namely, the compensation of victims of wrongdoing). It is hard to see how one could coherently regard this as acceptable, and yet regard it as unacceptable to inflict on the same individuals treatment which we can foresee would make other people suffer if it were imposed on them, in order to achieve goals to which these individuals

---

[25] We might think that a form of treatment's being is burdensome means there is (at least *prima facie*) a *reason* for not imposing it, even if it does not follow that we have a duty not to impose it. But this point would not count very strongly against versions of the expressive view which hold (as Bennett and Metz do) that societies have a duty to punish. For this duty would presumably outweigh these reasons against imposing burdensome treatment.

might not consent. Surely, the only way in which the fact that a form of treatment would foreseeably cause other individuals like the offender to suffer could be morally relevant is that the fact that it would cause those other individuals to suffer is very good evidence for the claim that this treatment would foreseeably make the offender suffer. If this can, in fact, be morally acceptable – as Boonin and Hanna think – then it seems as though the intentional inflicting of burdensome treatment on individuals to achieve valuable goals can also be acceptable.

5   Quarantine and the involuntary detainment of the mentally ill

Hanna argues that the existence of cases of burdensome treatment which are not punishment, such as quarantine and involuntary detainment of the mentally ill, shows that in characterizing punishment as harsh treatment, we think of harshness as involving an intention to cause suffering. Quarantine and the involuntary hospitalization of the mentally ill are not punishment because they do not involve an intention to cause suffering. [26]

There are at least two ways of denying that these are cases of punishment without accepting Hanna's view. One is derived from the account of punishment I outlined in the first paragraph of the paper; the other on considerations peculiar to the expressive view.

Both quarantine and involuntary confinement could take forms which would be found burdensome by a typical individual of the kind on whom it is being imposed. So for me, they would count as harsh treatment. However, it does not follow that they are forms of punishment.

On the account of punishment outlined at the beginning of the chapter, a form of harsh treatment only constitutes punishment if it is imposed as a response to wrongdoing. [27] If so, then quarantine is not (normally) a form of punishment, since it is not normally imposed as a response to wrongdoing. [28]

In considering involuntary hospitalization of the mentally ill, we should distinguish between two different kinds of situation. In one an individual is confined on the grounds that they represent a danger to themselves or

---

[26] Hanna 2008 pp. 127–8.

[27] As I say in Section 6, the word 'response' is normatively freighted here.

[28] It is also not, typically, imposed by the right kind of authority. Still, we can imagine cases where quarantine was judicially imposed which would still not be punishment.

others. (In the UK, cases of this sort typically require the invoking of Section 2 of the Mental Health Act and the signature of more than one doctor.) Cases of this sort should not be regarded as cases of punishment because, like quarantine, they do not occur as a response to wrongdoing.[29]

The case of individuals who are sentenced to long-term confinement to secure psychiatric institutions after having committed a crime is more complicated. Such treatment is typically, in my terms, harsh; *ex hypothesi* it is a response to wrongdoing; and it is imposed by an appropriate authority. Unlike the cases of quarantine and of sectioning under the Mental Health Act, it is not immediately obvious that these should not be counted as cases of punishment. We should take seriously the possibility that these cases do involve punishment – maybe punishment masquerading as, or accompanied by, something else. If they do, we may, rightly, be troubled by them.

Alternatively, one might argue that contrary to first appearances, these kinds of cases do not involve inflicting harsh treatment *in response* to wrongdoing. It is certainly true that in these kinds of cases, some apparent wrongdoing is the occasion of the imposition of harsh treatment. But there are good reasons for distinguishing between what occasions harsh treatment and what the hard treatment in question is a response to. What occasions the harsh treatment is a breach of some social norm, which initiates a judicial and medical process, which results in confinement. However, it is arguable that any part of the harsh treatment which is not properly viewed as punishment is only legitimately imposed in cases where the individual is judged to be less than fully culpable because of their mental condition. In other words the imposition of non-punitive harsh treatment would typically be accompanied by a form of official recognition that this harsh treatment is precisely *not* a response to wrongdoing but something else instead, such as a precaution against future danger.[30]

---

[29] Hearings under the Mental Health Act, or similar legislation in other countries might be regarded as having some kind of quasi-judicial aspect to them. But, importantly, doctors are not asked to make any judgment as to whether there has been any kind of wrongdoing, but only of whether an individual is dangerous or not.

[30] We can infer that it is not a response to wrongdoing from the fact that we would not judge the response mistaken if we found that the individual who is being confined is not culpable. Culpability is a necessary condition for wrongdoing but not for breach of a social norm. (The significant difference here then is between culpable wrongdoing and (mere, perhaps non-culpable) breach of a social norm, not between 'response' and 'occasion'. I thank an anonymous referee for insisting on this clarification.)

A second reason for thinking that standard cases of quarantine and confinement of the mentally ill do not constitute punishment can be extracted from views held by at least some of the expressivists against whom Hanna is arguing – and in particular by Feinberg and Duff. Duff and Feinberg both hold that even where harsh treatment is a response to wrongdoing, it only constitutes punishment if it either serves the right kind of expressive purpose or is intended to do so.[31] It is plausible that neither quarantine nor involuntary confinement of the mentally ill meet this condition. If they did meet this condition we would be rightly troubled by them, as we would in the case of involuntary confinement of the mentally ill imposed as a response to wrongdoing by non-judicial authorities.

6   Arrest, self-defense and just war

Several other examples of behavior, which one might take to involve inflicting harsh treatment as a response to wrongdoing, are also not plausibly viewed as forms of punishment.[32] Here are four: the arrest and pre-trial detention of criminals; self defense; the defense of others against attacks on them; just warfare; and court-ordered forcible resti-tution of property by offenders. None of them should be regarded as problematic by someone who thinks that expressive goals form part of the definition of punishment.[33]

Arrest and pre-trial detention of suspected criminals certainly involves treatment which I call harsh. However, these are arguably not responses to wrongdoing, but to reasonable suspicions of wrongdoing, since the innocent can (legitimately) be arrested. One might object that by the same token that post-trial incarceration is not a response to wrongdoing either, since one can be found guilty and incarcerated even if one is in fact innocent. However, the cases are disanalogous.

To see why, notice that the word 'response' is normatively freighted here, in a way that other similar words (such as the word 'reaction' on some readings) are not. If I am responding to X, I must be acting in a way that is appropriately sensitive to whether X has occurred – for example by

---

[31] Feinberg 1965; Duff 2009. For more about what the right kind of expressive purpose might be, see Section 8. (As one anonymous reader noted, we might think that involuntary detention of the mentally ill expresses concern for the safety of the community.)

[32] As an anonymous reader suggested.

[33] An alternative response, which I do not explore here for reasons of space, would be to argue that while these may be cases of punishment, they are cases of punishment which are not justified or justifiable in virtue of their status as acts of punishment.

being prepared to treat my actions as mistaken and to make due reparation for them if it can be shown that X has not occurred, and so on.

This explains how the cases of pre-trial and post-trial incarceration differ. Someone who is found guilty, imprisoned, and then shown to be innocent is thereby shown to have been wronged.[34] Someone who is found innocent after being arrested and detained need not be: if they have been detained on grounds of reasonable suspicion, they cannot claim to have been wrongfully arrested. So we have some grounds for saying that post-trial incarceration is a response to wrongdoing, whereas pre-trial detention is not: in cases where there has been no wrongdoing, we take it that we have, *for that very reason*, responded wrongly in the case of post-trial incarceration, whereas we do not automatically take this to be the case in situations where there has been pre-trial arrest and confinement, in situations where there are reasonable grounds to suspect wrongdoing but no actual wrongdoing.

It is harder to argue that self-defense is a response to something other than wrongdoing than it is to argue that arrest and pre-trial confinement are.[35] We might want to say that in situations where I respond defensively to something which does not involve wrongdoing, I should take my response to be mistaken. This is not clear-cut: perhaps justifiable self-defense only requires a credible threat of wrongdoing, not actual wrongdoing. However, we should not depend upon this point.

The minimal account of punishment from Section 1 provides one kind of ground for denying that self-defense is a form of punishment. On that account, punishment needs to be inflicted by an appropriate authority. Still, there might be cases of self-defense by figures such as policemen and judges, who one might take to be appropriate authorities. To deal with such cases, we might say that, in cases where they are defending themselves, policemen and judges are not acting in their capacity as appropriate authorities. However, this response requires an adequate account of what an appropriate authority is. There is some risk that the account might turn out to be circular: it might end up saying, for example, that an appropriate authority is one which can punish justifiably.

The suggestion that punishment only counts as such if imposed by an appropriate authority also fails to explain why some cases of the

---

[34] In civilized jurisdictions this is publicly acknowledged.

[35] The case of self-defense provides no support for a conception of punishment that involves an intention to harm. A self-defensive action may involve an intention to harm, without ceasing to be self-defense (It may be that I can only defend myself effectively by inflicting pain on my attacker, for example.).

use of force in the defense of others should not be counted as punishment. Some defensive uses of force appear to be imposed by appropriate authorities. A policeman may be authorized to use force to protect innocent bystanders; and a member of an army may be authorized to use force in response to wrongful invasion of a piece of territory. One might also appeal to traditional forms of Just War Theory for further examples of the use of force, imposed by a rightful authority, in response to wrongdoing, which should not be counted as forms of punishment.

Even if we think that arrest, pre-trial detention, some forms of self- and other-defense and justifiable war should be regarded as forms of harsh treatment which are responses to wrongdoings imposed by appropriate authorities, expressivists – or at least expressivists such as Duff and Feinberg – need not be committed to regarding them as forms of punishment. For they can argue that none of these forms of behavior are supposed to have the kinds of expressive function which are essential to punishment. This is clearest in the case of arrest and pre-trial detention. Since it has not been established, until a trial has occurred, that the arrested and detained individual has committed a wrong the arrest and detention of a suspected wrongdoer cannot properly be supposed to express social condemnation of the wrong which has been committed.[36] Similar points might be made about the defense of self or others: we can only describe behavior in this way if it is intended to prevent harm to self or others. To the extent that it is intended to do more than this, we should regard it as something else. (In some cases, as when a looter in a flooded a city is shot to 'show what's what', we may have is a case of something which is, in fact, unauthorized, and hence illegitimate punishment.)[37]

---

[36] So-called perp walks are, therefore, problematic, since they seem to have the sort of expressive function which is constitutive of punishment, but they come after an arrest, not a finding of guilt. For further discussion, see Chapter 6.

[37] If it is part of our notion of punishment that it be imposed by an appropriate authority, can we make any sense of the idea of illegitimate punishment? Yes. I can have authority in a particular area, yet exercise it in ways that go beyond what is legitimate. (I may have authority to punish students in my class for plagiarism. But if I whip a plagiarist, what I do is illegitimate: I have exceeded my authority. Still, it is punishment.) Notice that we need not concede that everything we can reasonably describe as a case of illegitimate punishment is a case of punishment. Sometimes, illegitimate punishment is no more a case of something that is genuinely punishment, but illegitimate than a fake banknote is a particular species of banknote. (The 'masquerades of punishment' mentioned in note 32 are 'fake' in exactly the same way as a fake banknote is fake.)

7   Court-ordered restitution

This leaves forced restitution, which could constitute harsh treatment on my account: it is a response to a wrongdoing and could be imposed by a court, which would constitute an appropriate authority. If forced restitution is a form of punishment, as some think, there is no objection here.[38] However, legal systems which allow for the possibility of court-ordered restitution often treat it as a civil rather than a criminal matter: judgments on claims for restitution may only require a judgment based on a 'balance of probabilities' standard of proof rather than proof beyond reasonable doubt. But perhaps a revisionary response is appropriate: since court-ordered restitution is a form of punishment, we should in fact require a criminal level of proof here.

What makes a particular standard of proof appropriate? If a court's task is only to determine how the burdens brought about by a particular action should be distributed, a probabilistic judgment seems appropriate. However, if the court's task is in part to express a moral judgment on behalf of society, it is important that it be shown that the wrong being condemned has been committed. The converse is also plausible: we are entitled to take the fact that a case is decided on the basis of a balance of probabilities as a reason for thinking that the judgment is not intended to have a communicative purpose and thus that it does not constitute a form of punishment on the expressive conception. We might then argue that some cases of court-ordered restitution – as that is currently understood – are not cases of punishment precisely because they are not intended to serve the expressive goals which punishment, properly so-called, is supposed to have.

Boonin has suggested that existing practices of civil restitution might be extended to cover cases where restitution needs to take non-monetary forms to deal with so-called secondary harms to victims.[39] In many such cases, it may not permissible or feasible for someone other than the wrongdoer to undertake restitution on the wrongdoer's behalf. For example, Boonin suggests that a highly successful burglar might be required to restore his victims' previous sense of security by wearing a device which allowed the police to monitor his location. Clearly no-one else could do this on behalf of the burglar. This 'non-substitutability' feature suggests that here we would not have a purely civil matter here.

---

[38] Cholbi 2010. (I thank Nathan Hanna for drawing my attention to this piece in correspondence.)

[39] Boonin 2008 pp. 231–5.

If so, this would be a reason for treating these cases as requiring proof 'beyond reasonable doubt', and of having an expressive purpose which makes them, *contra* Boonin, into punishment.

8   Have we saved expressivism?

I have argued that harsh treatment need not be intended to cause suffering. I now need to argue that punishment can be expressive in the ways expressivists require in virtue of being harsh (and not, for example, only in virtue of being intended to cause suffering).[40]

On a denunciatory view, the purpose of the harsh treatment that punishment involves is for a society to communicate to its members that certain norms are in force and transgressions against them are viewed seriously.[41] A form of treatment need not be intended to cause suffering in order to have this role. A response to wrongdoing can be understood in the right way even if it does not actually cause suffering. It may be enough that it is the sort of thing which members of the society would typically take to be burdensome. In this case it need not be part of our intention in punishing someone that they are made to suffer. We need only intend that the punishment be harsh in the sense I have outlined. To see this, consider our responses to a citizen who, knowing that certain kinds of judicial response to wrongdoing were, in my terms 'harsh', concerned themselves with the question of whether particular, named individuals were actually being caused suffering. It is plausible that, absent special circumstances, we would find this troubling: it seems unduly voyeuristic.

Something similar is true on Bennett's view. For Bennett, punishment involves the expression, on the part of society of certain 'reactive attitudes'.[42] But, claims Bennett, the state has no legitimate interest in whether the individual has actually repented.[43] Importantly we can express reactive attitudes in conventional ways; and inflicting treatment which is, in my sense, harsh, can be seen as doing just this. There is no further requirement that the treatment be intended to cause suffering to the particular individual who is being punished.

On Duff's view matters are more complicated. Duff holds that punishment can only be justified if the sorts of treatment which punishment

---

[40] I thank an anonymous reader for suggesting that I make this explicit here.
[41] Wringe 2006.
[42] Bennett 2008 pp. 247–74.
[43] Ibid. pp. 196–7.

characteristically involve are aimed at making an offender experience remorse for their wrongdoing.[44] Since it is unpleasant to suffer remorse, one might think that if we inflict harsh treatment on individuals with the goal of causing them to feel remorse we are intentionally causing suffering. If I do A in order to bring about B, then I have intentionally brought B about. So it might seem that the characterization of harshness offered here does not enable Duff's view to escape Hanna's criticism.

Perhaps this is simply a reason to prefer Bennett's version of the expressive view to Duff's. However, as I noted in Section 2, Hanna's critique of expressivism is based on the idea that even if punishment has expressive goals, it is possible to achieve these goals without engaging in treatment which is intended to cause suffering.[45] If one of the goals of punishment is to cause people to experience remorse, and if doing something in order to cause them to experience remorse is intentionally causing them suffering, then there is, in fact, no way of achieving this goal without intentionally causing them suffering. In short, on this line of argument, Hanna has no case against Duff.

Anticipating this point Hanna suggests that a communicative theorist of Duff's stripe see the goal of punishment as being to cause the offender to acknowledge their wrongdoing rather than make them feel remorse. The important point here for Hanna's purposes is that, as he emphasizes, one can recognize that one has done wrong without suffering remorse.[46] Duff might not accept this reformulation of his views, on the grounds that a recognition that one has done wrong which does not involve some sort of suffering would not achieve the goals which remorse can achieve. (One might regard the suggested form of recognition as constituting a form of sociopathy where serious wrongdoing was concerned.) However, even if Duff accepts the proposed reformulation, Hanna's critique still fails. If punishment involves treatment which is, in my terms, harsh and which is aimed not at causing remorse, but at bringing about a recognition of wrongdoing (with remorse as, presumably,

---

[44] Duff sometimes writes in ways that suggest that this is part of the definition of punishment, and sometimes in ways which do not make it definitional but which do make it integral to the justification of punishment. For an example of the latter see Duff 2001 pp. xiv–xv. For an example of the former see Duff 2009.

[45] Hanna 2008 p. 143.

[46] Ibid. p. 144.

an inessential, but perhaps frequent by-product), then it need not involve an intention to cause suffering after all.

9 Types of offender: some problems

One might think my account of harsh treatment fails because it relies on the unacceptably vague idea of a typical individual of the same kind as the offender. I have said nothing about which of the ways in which individuals are similar to one another are relevant to deciding whether a given form of treatment is harsh in a given case. Should we consider – for example – the 'type' of an offender to consist of all individuals who are convicted of the same crime? Or all individuals accused of the same kind? Or all individuals convicted of a particular crime of a particular socio-economic class? Or all individuals in the society?

Although the account of harshness that I have given is indeed under-specified in this respect, this is not a significant problem. For the purpose of giving an account of harshness which is acceptable to the theorist of punishment it is important that there should be *at least one* way of explicating the notion of harshness on which a punishment's being harsh does not entail that it be imposed with the intention of causing suffering. This will be true if there is *one* possible way of dividing offenders up into classes that have typical members. If there is more than one, then so much the better.

For practical purposes, matters are different: we may find that there is a difference between the kinds of punishments that we impose if we take as our standard for harshness what would be found burdensome by a typical member of the society doing the punishing, or what would be found burdensome by a typical individual convicted of a particular crime, or by a typical individual of a particular social class. (The problem only arises when there are noticeable differences between what typical members of these types would find burdensome. There need not always be. For example, there may be no difference between what a typical member of the class of individuals convicted of an offense would find burdensome and what a typical member of the class of individuals accused of that offense would find burdensome.) However it is not immediately obvious that philosophical considerations, as opposed to political or practical ones, ought to solve this problem.

The appeal to typical individuals in my characterization of harsh-ness might be thought to risk the imposition of sentences which were disproportionately light or disproportionately severe in their impact on a particular individual. For an individual might be unusually resilient in the face of certain treatment or unusually prone to suffer from it. In other words they might be individuals who suffer either much more or much less than the typical individuals of their type. (This might matter simply on grounds of fairness; but an expressive theorist might also see it as something that could undermine the expressive goals of punishment.)

How far this is a problem on a practical level would depend on how we assign offenders to 'types'. So we might think our assignment of individuals to types should be done in such a way as to minimize the extent to which problems of this sort arise. Unfortunately, it seems to be built into the very structure of the account of harshness which I have offered that cases like this should be able to arise – that is, that there might be differences between what a particular individual finds burdensome and what an individual of their type might find burdensome. Even if we overlook this, it seems unlikely to be possible in practice to divide individuals into types that correspond to the exact degree to which they would find any particular kind of punishment burdensome.

Similar problems arise for any punitive regime that attempts to assign sentences on the basis of general guidelines. Since any reasonably realistic punitive regime would do so, my account of punishment faces no greater problems than any other account would. Still, the objection might be sharpened by suggesting that, whereas we ought to regard this as an imperfection in our actual sentencing regimes resulting from practical limitations on our knowledge of the circumstances of particular offenders, the account of punishment I have been offering requires it.

However it is not clear that a good account of punishment should yield a justification for perfectly tailored punishments. The fact that mine does not is a strength, not a weakness. It reflects the fact that in punishing me, the state should treat me impersonally. As Bennett has argued, there seems to be something worryingly illiberal about the idea that the state should be concerned with the state of my individual soul. One might regard this point as a problem for any version of the communicative view. But as we have seen, Bennett argues this is not correct.[47] The communicative theorist can regard the state's imposition of punishments as providing a way for offenders to undergo something which can formally be regarded as being a form of penance.

---

[47] Bennett 2006, 2008 pp. 196–7.

If so, what matters is not whether an individual actually suffers, but whether they undergo something that would typically be regarded as burdensome.[48]

Advocates of communicative theories of punishment sometimes argue that their accounts are preferable to consequentialist accounts because consequentialist accounts treat punished individuals as means to an end. One might think the account of punishment that I have offered is open to a similar worry. For the account seems to require us to treat individuals who are punished not *as* individuals, but as representatives of particular types, and thus perhaps, not as ends in themselves, but as mere means.

The Kantian prohibition on treating individuals as means to an end is best understood either as a prohibition on treating them in ways those could not consent to; or as a prohibition on treating them in a way which does not respect their rational nature. Neither understanding rules out the possibility of regarding punished offenders as representatives of a type. There is no reason why a penitent offender could not regard themselves as being appropriately treated as a member of a type – particularly if they understood the rationale for that treatment as being along the lines which a communicative theorist of punishment would suggest.

Treating an individual as a member of a type involves no disrespect for their rational nature. A rational being is one that is capable of recognizing and responding in ways that are sensitive to the force of rational considerations. But different types of rational beings can recognize and be sensitive to such considerations in distinctively different ways. Recognizing that an individual is responsive to rational considerations in one way rather than another may well be a way of regarding them as a representative of a type. Seeing someone as a rational being of a particular kind is not inconsistent with – or even in tension with – seeing them as a rational being: rather it requires it.

---

[48] What is true of the state may not be true of other kinds of individuals or institutions who have the right to punish individuals under certain circumstances, such as parents, schools or religious communities. This will strike some defenders of expressivism as a problem insofar as they favor an account of what punishment is that applies both to state and non-state punishments. However, I do not think that allowing for a slight difference in what we take punishment to be is especially counter-intuitive here, particularly when weighed against the benefits of having an account of state punishment which escapes Hanna's objection.

10   Theory and practice

I have claimed that there is a useful conceptual distinction to be made between punishment's being harsh and its being intended to cause suffering to the individual on whom it is inflicted; and that Hanna's and Boonin's critiques of expressive theories of punishment fail because they ignores this distinction. However, one might argue that although there is a conceptual distinction between punishment's being harsh and its being intended to cause suffering, there is no practical difference: any institution which reliably inflicts harsh treatment will either do so by intentionally inflicting harm on those it treats harshly, or will do so in ways which involve someone intentionally inflicting harm on someone else.

It is plausible, given my characterization of harsh treatment, that no institution could inflict harsh treatment on a regular basis without it being foreseeable that some individuals will be caused to suffer. But we can distinguish between an outcome's being foreseen and its being intended. One way of doing so is to ask what an agent's response would be if the foreseen event did not occur. Suppose, then, that the miraculous does occur: wrongdoers are treated in a way which would typically cause suffering to individuals like them – but – on a one in a million chance – they do not suffer. If the inflicting of suffering on these individuals is intentional, we should regard the punishment as having failed. And if it is possible to cause these individuals suffering by making them undergo treatment which is idiosyncratically designed in such a way to cause them suffering even if it would not do so to a typical individual like them, we should prefer to do this than inflict treatment which is – on the view of harshness defended here – harsh.

Whatever one might think of institutions which treated people in these ways, they would be very unlike our existing punitive institutions. So it does seem possible to distinguish, in this case, between suffering being inflicted in a way that is foreseen and suffering being inflicted in a way that is intentional. And this is what is required to meet the objection.

Someone might nonetheless refuse to accept a difference between treating an individual in a way that involves intentionally inflicting suffering on them and one which involves doing so foreseeably. In defending the viability of the conception of harsh treatment outlined here, I have only claimed that the intended/foreseen distinction makes a moral difference in a very restricted range of cases. One might accept everything said in this section and still think that in many cases there is

no significant difference between inflicting harm on someone intentionally and doing so foreseeably. However, anyone who agrees with Duff
in seeing the legitimacy of punishment as resting on the nature of the
relationship between punishing institutions and punished individuals,
and in requiring that it be one that treats the punished as individuals,
is likely to find the distinction between intentionally treating someone
in a particular way and doing so foreseeably to be morally significant.
Refusing to accept the distinction in this context risks begging the question against many advocates of the communicative view.[49]

---

[49] I thank Nathan Hanna and two anonymous readers for helpful comments
on this chapter.

3
Punishment As Expression: Who? What? To Whom?

1 Introduction

In Chapter 2, I argued that we have good reasons for adopting an account of punishment on which it is essential to something's constituting punishment that it be harsh treatment with an expressive dimension. However, this characterization of punishment raises a number of important questions. Two seem particularly obvious: an expressive account of punishment should tell us what punishment is supposed to express and who it is supposed to express it to. As we saw in Chapter 2, advocates of different versions of expressivism have answered this second question in a number of different ways: some have supposed that the primary audience for the messages that punishment involves are offenders, and others have supposed that it is society at large.

The answers to these questions seem likely to have a significant bearing on one another. Our view of what punishment can, and should, express is likely to be linked to our view of who it is supposed to be expressing it to. However, I shall argue in this chapter that we are unlikely to be able to give a satisfactory answer to either question unless we address a question that advocates of expressive theories of punishment rarely address head on: the question of who or what it is that is expressing the messages that are involved in punishment. I shall also argue that answering this question casts significant light on questions about how punishment is to be justified.

For the purposes of this chapter I shall focus on what I labeled in the introduction the 'paradigmatic case' of punishment: that in which a member of a political community is punished by the legitimate representatives of that community for offenses against laws made in the right way by duly constituted legislative bodies. In calling this the 'paradigmatic case' I do not intend to suggest that instances of punishment which do not fit this pattern are uncommon or unimportant (indeed, in the second half of this book I shall discuss several kinds of punishment which do not fit this paradigm). The point is rather that these are cases where questions about the nature and justifiability of punishment are most easily answered. Expressive theorists need to be able to give an account of punishment that seems plausible in cases of this sort if they are to have any chance of extending their view to cover non-paradigmatic cases.

2   The subject of penal communication

The question of who or what might be expressing the attitudes or messages which the expressive theorist takes to be embodied in punishment may seem obvious. On many accounts, it will be the agent or authority who is inflicting punishment on an offender. However, although this answer may seem straightforward when we are considering cases of what one might call 'private punishment, such as that of a parent punishing their child, it seems less clear when we are concerned with the case of legal punishment. This is because it is not immediately obvious in the case of legal punishment who exactly we should see as being the agent that inflicts punishment.

We might at first think that the agent is the individual who inflicts on the convicted offender the hardship whose imposition constitutes the punishment: the jailer or prison-warder for someone who is imprisoned; the executioner in cases of capital punishment, and so on. However, this view is clearly unsatisfactory. For one thing, the jailer or executioner may not actually have the attitudes which this account requires them to have: the executioner may see themselves as someone who is merely doing their job and the prison-warder may privately think of his charges in ways which do not reflect official attitudes to wrongdoing. The attitudes of the officials who are responsible for inflicting duly imposed penal measures seem irrelevant to the question of whether the individuals on whom this treatment is inflicted are correctly described as being punished.[1] The same points apply to the judge who convicts an

---

[1] They might conceivably be relevant if we thought that harsh treatment must involve an intention to cause suffering, and if we thought this was more likely to occur if the officials involved had this kind of attitude. But we saw in Chapter 2 that this conception of harshness was unsatisfactory.

offender and imposes a sentence: he or she may impose a sentence while taking the law which requires him to do so to be morally unjustifiable.[2]

Feinberg speaks of 'society' expressing reprobation and resentment through the legal system.[3] On one interpretation this seems as mistaken as the view that punishment expresses reprobation on the part of either the judge or the prison-warder. Even if a law or a form of punishment is unpopular or widely thought to be unjust, it can continue to be in force. Its reprobative function may be undiminished. However, there is another interpretation which seems more plausible. We might think of 'society' or 'the public' not merely as a collection of individuals, but as a kind of collective agent.

The idea that 'society' is a collective agent is liable to excite two kinds of skepticism. One is about the idea of collective agency in general. The second is about the claim that 'society' should be regarded as a collective agent. I have little sympathy for the first kind of skepticism, but some for the second. In recent years, a number of philosophers have developed detailed and careful theories of collective agency.[4] They have argued that sentences such as 'Acme Corporation is trying to increase its market share' and 'The United Kingdom will not withdraw from its treaty obligations' should be understood literally;[5] they have pointed to our practice of holding collective bodies legally and morally responsible for their actions;[6] and they have argued that there is, in general, no straightforward way to translate statements about the actions, beliefs and intentions of groups into statements about the actions, beliefs and intentions of individuals who make up those groups.[7]

Those who think that the idea of collective agency makes sense typically place fairly strong constraints on the kinds of groups that can be considered collective agents. They may require that the group in question have some kind of collective decision procedure which will make it possible to identify which acts undertaken by members of the group constitute actions of the group itself;[8] or that group members engage in certain kinds of 'joint commitment' to behave in certain ways; or, less

---

[2] I'm grateful to Lars Vinx for a last-minute comment which influenced the way I phrased this point.

[3] Feinberg 1965 p. 399.

[4] French 1984; Gilbert 1989; List and Pettit 2011; Stilz 2011.

[5] French 1984.

[6] Pettit 2007.

[7] List and Pettit 2011.

[8] French 1984.

ambitiously, that they have certain kinds of interlocking intentions.[9] We may then wish to distinguish between groups that meet whichever conditions a particular theory thinks are necessary for joint action and those that do not. If, following Margaret Gilbert, we call groups of the second sort 'mere aggregates', then the second sort of skepticism I have mentioned might be characterized as holding that society is a mere aggregate.[10]

Someone might take 'society' to refer to the group of people living in a particular state. We might plausibly take this to be a mere aggregate. However, it is much less plausible that the state is a mere aggregate. States appear to be paradigmatic examples of the kinds of group which theorists of collective action have wanted to regard as collective agents. They have formal decision procedures which enable us to distinguish between – say – acts undertaken by the British Prime Minister which are acts of the United Kingdom (such as signing a treaty) and acts which are merely the acts of David Cameron (such as leaving his children at a restaurant). They are the kinds of entity that can be held morally responsible; they are also the kinds of entity that can have legal standing (although, under international law as currently constituted they cannot be the subjects of criminal responsibility). This suggests that if we are to adopt an expressive theory of legal punishment, which should see the messages expressed as being messages expressed by the state, considered as a collective agent.[11]

3 Penal communication – the simplified Nozickian view

What is the content of penal communication? In his groundbreaking discussion of expressivism Feinberg suggests that the expressive function of punishment involves a 'fusing' of two separate elements, which he calls 'resentment' and 'reprobation'. Feinberg defines 'reprobation' as a 'stern judgment of disapproval' and resentment as any one of a range of 'vengeful attitudes'.[12]

It may at first seem tempting to align these two distinct components with two distinct things that one might think of punishment as expressing: one the one hand a purely cognitive attitude, and on the

---

[9] Bratman 1992, 2007; Kutz 2000.
[10] Gilbert 1989.
[11] Thus answering a worry about expressivism discussed at considerable length by Adler 2000.
[12] Feinberg 1965 p. 399.

other, an emotion with no propositional content. However, this way of seeing things seems problematic: it seems to presuppose – controversially, and in my view implausibly – that emotions are best seen as having no propositional content, and that the classes of cognitive states and emotions are entirely disjoint.[13] It also does some violence to the exact form in which Feinberg expresses his point, insofar as he specifies that the judgment involved in reprobation should be 'stern'. This at least suggests some form of emotional attitude. Furthermore, anything appropriately described as a 'vengeful attitude' is likely to have some propositional content.

This suggests that whatever is communicated in punishment will involve some kind of propositional content. However, Feinberg does not tell us a great deal about how we might pin down the expressive content of punishment more precisely. Nor does he say much to tell us how it is that punishment can be taken as expressive of anything at all. However, these issues have been addressed, in some detail, by Robert Nozick.[14] Nozick draws on an account of meaning put forward by H.P. Grice, who suggests that for someone to mean some proposition p by an act, they must intend that some other agent

(i)   come to believe that p;
(ii) recognize the intention involved in (i);
(iii) have as part of their reason for believing p the recognition involved in (ii).[15]

Grice illustrates his point by considering the case of someone's using a car's indicator light to signal that one is turning. Suppose I switch on my car's indicator light in order to signal that I plan to turn left. My action means that I plan to turn left if it is true that I intend someone to come to believe that I am turning left, intend that they recognize that I intend them to believe that I am planning to turn left, and intend that they should have as part of their reason for believing that I am planning to turn left their recognition of my intention that they should believe that I am planning to turn left.

Grice's account of meaning is controversial: many authors (starting with Grice himself) have sought to produce counter-examples. Many

---

[13] Wringe 2015.
[14] Nozick 1981.
[15] Grice 1989.

of the counter-examples which have been put forward are instances of actions which appear to have a particular meaning without satisfying these conditions. If these counter-examples succeed, they show that Grice's conditions do not provide necessary conditions for somebody to mean something by something. However, we need not worry about such cases. For our purposes it will be enough that Grice's conditions provide sufficient conditions for meaning. It is much harder to produce counter-examples to this claim.[16]

Nozick claims that many instances of punishment involve cases where an agent inflicting a penalty on an offender intends that the offender come to believe that their action was wrong and that they should recognize that the punishment has been inflicted on them in order that they should come to believe that their action was wrong. He also suggests, more controversially that they may involve inflicting pain with the intention that the offender recognize that the punishment has been inflicted on them in order to make them believe their action was wrong and have this recognition as part of their reason for believing that their action was wrong. If Nozick is correct, then it will indeed be the case that these acts of punishment are acts that express to an offender that a particular act is wrong. And, if we think that acts of punishment typically satisfy these conditions, and that they are carried out because they satisfy these conditions, we may find it plausible to conclude that punishment has the function of expressing reprobation to an offender.

Nozick's own view of punishment differs from this in certain respects: in particular he takes punishment to have the function of communicating not only that a certain act is wrong, but that it is wrong to a certain degree. So I shall call the view I have outlined the 'Simplified Nozickian View'. It has two salient elements. First, it says that punishment communicates that a certain act is wrong. Secondly, it suggests that the primary recipient of this message is the offender who is punished.

---

[16] Searle 1969 might seem to be a counter-example: he gives the example of an American soldier using a line of German poetry which he remembers but does not know the meaning of in order to persuade some Germans that he is a German. But it is not clear this is a counter-example: if we distinguish between sentence meaning and utterance meaning, it seems plausible that the meaning of the American's utterance, though not of the sentence he uses, is precisely that he is German. For further helpful discussion see Morris 2000 pp. 248–70.

4   Problems for the Simplified Nozickian view (I)

It is not immediately clear whether the Simplified Nozickian View is consistent with the claim that punishment involves the expression of messages by states. If it is, states must be able to have complex communicative intentions of the sort which Grice's account requires.

There are many accounts of collective action which suggest that they can. For example, on Margaret Gilbert's account, a group can have a collective intention by committing itself to act as a body in a certain respect.[17] While the notion of acting as a body may require further elucidation, the structure of Gilbert's account does not appear to place any strong constraints on the kinds of intentions which collective agents can have. In particular, it does not appear to preclude collective bodies from having the sorts of intention which the Simplified Nozickian View specifies.

On Peter French's account of collective agency, a collective's capacity for agency depends on the existence of a corporate decision structure which specifies which actions are to count as actions of the collective.[18] Corporate decision structures may include a number of different elements. They may provide for certain kinds of actions to be actions of the corporation when voted on by a majority of the board of the directors; others to be actions of the corporation when voted on by shareholders; and others to be actions of the corporation when carried out by designated individuals (such as the CEO or the Chief Financial Officer) acting within particular, clearly defined fields. This model of collective agency may seem more plausibly applicable to the actions of a state than Gilbert's. For our purposes what is most significant about French's model is that it allows us to see such procedures as Parliament's approving a law criminalizing certain kinds of behavior and imposing certain kinds of sentence to count as expressing the intentions of the state.[19]

Some philosophers might accept that states can, in principle, have the kinds of intention that French suggests, but deny that they should be regarded as doing so in practice. For example, someone might suggest that in voting to approve a law which criminalizes a certain kind of behavior and imposes penalties for it, the state is simply expressing its intention to prevent behavior of certain kinds and to institute measures which will deter people from acting in the way which they are trying to

---

[17] Gilbert 1989.
[18] French 1984.
[19] For another account of the state as a collective agent, see Stilz 2011.

prevent. Why should we understand states as doing any more than this when they adopt such measures? In particular, why we should interpret them as doing anything so specific as intending that offenders should come to believe that certain kinds of action are wrong, let alone that they should do so for particular reasons?

An advocate of an expressive theory of state punishment needs to answer this question. They can do so by pointing out that when a state criminalizes certain kinds of behavior, it does not bring a prohibition and a set of penalties into existence *ex nihilo*. Instead, it incorporates a new law into an existing body of criminal law and procedure which includes such things as rules of evidence; standard forms of criminal process; rules about circumstances under which a defendant is and is not responsible for certain actions to certain courts and under which responsibility – the requirement to answer for certain actions – does and does not give rise to liability (susceptibility to punishment); the requirement that certain facts meet a particular burden of proof (e.g., in English courts, the requirement that elements of a crime be proved by the prosecution beyond reasonable doubt, whereas the inapplicability of certain defenses need not be); and so on. [20]

We should take all of this into account in interpreting what legislatures are doing when they criminalize certain forms of behavior. Our task is not to discern what might have been in the heads of individual legislators when they voted on a particular measure, but to give the most coherent overall picture of what they might be doing when determining that a particular prohibition become part of criminal law. This leaves room for the possibility that the actions of the legislature embody a collective intention whose content is richer than that suggested by the objector. (Whether or not they should be interpreted as having the precise content which the Simplified Nozickian View requires them to have is another matter; I shall argue that they cannot.)

5 Problems for the simplified Nozickian view (II)

Some offenders might already believe their actions to be wrong. If they do, then punishment cannot succeed in causing them to come to believe that their action is wrong. Call this situation 'Failure to Receive'. Now consider an offender who believes their action was wrong, and an agent punishing them who knows they believe this. The agent inflicting punishment cannot cause an offender like this to come to believe that

---

[20] Duff 2007.

their action was wrong. Since an agent cannot intend to do something which they know to be impossible, they cannot even intend to cause the offender to believe that their action was wrong. Call this situation 'Failure to Transmit'.

Do situations like 'Failure to Receive' and 'Failure to Transmit' present problems for the Simplified Nozickian View? In 'Failure to Receive', punishment fails to achieve the end at which it aims. However, since things which have a function may also malfunction, the possibility of cases like this does not show that punishment does not have a communicative function.[21] 'Failure to Transmit' seems more serious: here it seems that punishment cannot achieve the end at which it aims.

Nevertheless, 'Failure to Transmit' seems to be less of a problem in the case of state-inflicted punishment than it might be in the case of 'private' or 'personal' punishment. For, as I have already argued, if we adopt an expressive account of state punishment we should see the state, as a collective agent, as the agent whose intentions are in question here. But we might think that it is unlikely that the state could come to be in a position to know, of a particular convicted offender, that they believed that what they were doing was morally wrong.

Here is a more serious problem. Grice's third condition on meaning requires that in meaning that p I should intend that an agent recognize that I intend them to come to believe that p and have their recognition that I intend them to come to believe that p be part of their reason for believing p. In the kinds of case Grice focuses on, the recognition presumably functions in the following way: the individual with whom I am communicating takes it to be the case that if I intend them to believe that p, then p. If so, then in order to have the third Gricean intention I must regard it as possible for the person with whom I am trying to communicate to have as part of their reason for believing that p my intention that they should believe that p.

In the case where I use my car indicator light to signal a turn, the fact that I intend you to believe that I am going to turn can be a reason for you to believe that I am going to turn. For the fact that I want you to believe that I am going to turn is, in standard cases, good evidence that

---

[21] If we think that punishment is justified by its fulfilling some communicative function, then cases where it fails to function as it should may present an obstacle to justifying punishment as an institution. However, we have not, thus far, been concerned with questions of justification: we shall consider them in more detail in the next chapter.

I am in fact going to turn. For it is evidence that I am going to make it the case that I turn.

Many cases of criminal wrongdoing involve what are called *mala in se*. In such cases, the law prohibits something which would be morally wrong even if it were not prohibited by law.[22] Murder and rape fall into this category. An agent's intention to make an offender believe that a *malum in se* is wrong cannot be a reason for that offender to believe it is wrong in the same way that my intention that you believe that I am going to turn can be a reason for you to believe that I am going to turn. No agent can make it the case that an action which is a *malum in se* is wrong: its wrongness does not depend on any agent. Furthermore, the fact that the wrongness of *mala in se* does not depend on the communicating agent should be obvious to anyone whose moral development is not so impaired as to raise questions as to whether they can be held criminally responsible at all.[23] So an offender cannot treat an agent's intention to make them believe that an action of this sort is wrong as evidence that the agent intends to make it true that it is wrong.

An agent's intention to make someone believe that something is wrong might be a reason for them to believe it is wrong in a different way. It might be evidence that the agent believes that it is wrong, and the fact that the agent believes it is wrong may be evidence that it is in fact wrong. Suppose I regard you as a moral authority and take myself to be morally adrift. I might then ask you what I should do in a particular situation. You might answer me in an indirect way. Reflecting on your answer, I might come to believe that you intend me to believe that the action I am contemplating is wrong and also to believe that you would not intend me to believe this unless the action was in fact wrong. Your intention in giving me an indirect answer might – though it need not – be to prompt me to reflect in precisely this way.[24]

In order for a case like this to constitute a case of Gricean communication, it seems to be necessary for you to intend to regard me as a reliable source of moral knowledge about whether p is wrong. Furthermore my ability to have this intention seems to depend on my at least taking it to be possible that you regard me as an authority on the question of

---

[22] The contrast here is with what are called *mala prohibita* – things which would not be wrong if there were no legal prohibition against them. (A standard example might be driving the wrong way up a one-way street.)

[23] It may not be true for psychopaths.

[24] It need not be: it may simply be I intended that you reflect on the matter in ways that give you independent reason for believing your action was wrong.

whether p is wrong. There are some cases of punishment where this seems both possible and appropriate. Consider, for example, a punishment of a young child by a parent, or a religious novice by their head of their order. However, there seems to be something more problematic about this idea when we consider the case of legal punishment. It is not clear whether states are reliable sources of moral knowledge; and there certainly seem to be good grounds for being skeptical as to whether they are. Furthermore there are many cases – perhaps a majority – where offenders will not regard the state as being a reliable source of moral knowledge. Furthermore, there may well be cases where we can know, of particular offenders, that they will not see the state as a source of reliable moral knowledge.

A slightly different worry is that offenders who do see the state as being a reliable source of moral knowledge have a distorted view of the state. We might, in other words, think that states do not, and should not, claim the kind of moral expertise that offenders would have to see them as having in order for the account in question to work. One reason for holding this would be commitment to a view on which liberal states are supposed to take a neutral view on substantive questions of value. However Joseph Raz and Antony Duff have argued that this is an unattractive conception of liberalism.[25] Nevertheless, even if we think it is appropriate for a liberal state to embody and promote certain values, we might still regard it as problematic to think of the state as being something which mature adult citizens should look to as a source of moral guidance.

Someone might respond that these points present no obstacle to the claim that punishment can involve the communication of reprobation. They might concede that on the Simplified Nozickian View, the punitive actions of the state can only mean what they should if the offender views the state in a certain light; and whether the state should in fact be viewed in this light is irrelevant.

This point is correct as far as it goes; but the verdict it suggests seems unduly sanguine. For the objection does seem to raise a difficult for anyone who hopes that attention to the communicative role of punishment will cast light on the justification of punishment. For on this account, punishment will only achieve the goals which it is supposed to achieve if it is seen in a distorted manner.[26]

---

[25] Raz 1986; Duff 2001.
[26] I am grateful to comments from Lars Vinx that prompted me to think about this issue in more depth than I might otherwise have done.

On an account of this sort, the state must be less than fully transparent to those over whom it claims authority. This may seem problematic in and of itself: the idea that a state should be transparent to its citizens is one that seems to have a certain moral plausibility which is independent of other considerations. But here are two further considerations which may convince those who are not independently moved. One is that states whose functioning requires them to be non-transparent seem likely to be prone to instability: what happens when individuals come to see that the justification of punishment requires a distorted understanding of the state?

A second is that the Gricean account seems to require not only that offenders see it in a distorted light but that the state must intend that these offenders see it in a distorted light: in other words it must intend to present itself deceptively. There is a good case for thinking that an agent who does so, whether individual or collective, will be adopting a maxim to which offenders could not possibly consent. In other words it seems as though on this kind of account the state will treat offenders as a means when it punishes them.[27]

6   Altering the message

My argument against the Simplified Nozickian View depended on features of the message which, on that conception, punishment was considered as carrying. So we might wonder whether the problem could be solved by adjusting this aspect of the view. I noted earlier that what I called the Simplified Nozickian View was not Nozick's own view. Nozick suggests the content of the message conveyed by a particular punitive act is not that a particular act was wrong, but that it was wrong to some particular degree. This suggestion is motivated by the observation that we typically think that a just system of punishment should obey some constraints of proportionality.

Does this slightly more sophisticated view escape the objection I have been drawing attention to? Unfortunately it does not. The problem we were concerned with was that in order for punishment to communicate the message that a criminal's act was wrong, the punishing authority had to be committed to intending that the offender see the punishing authority as morally authoritative. If the message is supposed to be

---

[27] This should seem particularly worrying to authors like Duff, who take it to be a significant point in favor of their view that it does not involve treating offenders as a means; see Duff 2001.

rather that a particular action is wrong to some particular degree, the punishing authority will have to intend that the offender see the state as authoritative about the degree to which their offense is morally wrong. This still requires that the punishing authority intend that the punished individual see the state as morally authoritative.

A more substantial suggestion along the same lines might be to suggest that the problem for the Simplified Nozickian View arises out of the fact that the message conveyed by punishment has a moral content.[28] So one might wonder whether the problem might be solved by suggesting that the message conveyed by punishment has a kind of content which is not moralized in this way. In Sections 9 and 10, I shall consider the possibility of punishment communicating non-moralized messages. However, as it stands, the suggestion seems incomplete: it is not clear how one might plausibly specify the non-moralized content of such a message. Could the message be that an offender has broken a law? If so then, punishment seems superfluous, since the process of trial and determination of guilt is supposed to specify this. Could it be that laws are enforced? If so, the content of the message seems circular in such a way as to suggest that the claim that punishment has an expressive dimension is unilluminating. In both cases, what seems to have gone missing is any sense that punishment communicates to an offender that they have done something which they ought not to have done.

7   Reconsidering the subject of penal communications

I have argued that the Simplified Nozickian View goes wrong because it requires offenders to see the state in a distorted light. The objection depends on the idea that the agent who is expressing a message via punishment is the state. It is natural to wonder whether the problem might be resolved if we took some agent other than the state to be the agent that is engaging in punishment. In his 2008 book *The Apology Ritual* Christopher Bennett makes a move of precisely this sort, suggesting, in effect, that punishment has an expressive dimension insofar as it allows an *offender* to express repentance in a ritualized and regulated form.

· One attraction of this view is that it makes sense of the somewhat counterintuitive idea that an offender might have a right to be punished. We might also think that it deals with the problem that I have raised for communicative views. If it is the offender rather than the state who is expressing something about the wrongness of their action, then we

---

[28] As Lars Vinx pointed out.

do not have to worry that the state may be setting itself up as a moral authority. However Bennett's view seems to face problems of its own.

Consider the question of what message we might take punishment to express on a view on which the subject of penal expression was the offender. A natural way of developing a view of this sort might be one on which, as on the Simplified Nozickian View, punishment expresses the claim that the offender's action was wrong. But it is hard to see how an offender's undergoing punishment could be expected to express to any audience a claim on the part of the offender that their action was wrong. Why should any audience recognize the offender's undergoing punishment as evidence that the offender wishes them to believe that their own action was wrong? And indeed how could they take the offender's undergoing that punishment as evidence that the offender wished them to recognize this?

Things are not much changed if we insist, as Bennett might, that what is communicated by the offender is not that their action was wrong, but that they themselves recognize that their action was wrong. The problem with views of this sort is not that it is difficult to see how an audience could understand an offender's undergoing punishment as involving an intent to communicate some particular message. It is that it is hard to see how they could understand it as involving the communication of any message from the offender at all. The problem is that in undergoing punishment the offender does not *do* anything at all. Since punishment is imposed upon an offender whether they like it or not, it does not seem to be something which involves any intentions on their part at all. And since this is a well-known fact about punishment, it does not seem as though any moderately well-informed audience could take it as embodying an intention of any sort.

Bennett might attempt to respond by drawing on a feature of his account which I have so far ignored, namely that punishment involves a ritualized and thus conventional form of expression. We might put the point like this. In an act of private repentance, I might voluntarily allow myself to undergo some form of harsh treatment as way of communicating that I understand that I have done something wrong. When I am punished by the state and undergo a similar form of harsh treatment, I undergo something which has as its conventional meaning that I recognize that I have done something wrong, and it does so because of the meaning that a similar sort of suffering would have if I were to choose it for myself.

This line of argument seems as though it might provide an adequate response to an objection which focuses on the fact that when an offender is punished they do not choose the form which their punishment takes. However it seems less powerful against a more powerful version of the same objection. The problem is that it is hard to see an offender's undergoing punishment as an event in which an offender expresses anything at all. When an offender is punished they typically do not *do* anything at all. As a consequence, they cannot be intending anything at all by undergoing punishment. *A fortiori* they cannot have the kind of Gricean intentions that they would need to have in order to be able to express anything by undergoing punishment.

Bennett might respond by suggesting that although an offender does not *do* anything just by being punished, their agency does come into play at other points. For example, we might emphasize that punishment is something which can be received willingly or unwillingly. However, although this is true, it seems unlikely to help Bennett here. For Bennett insists, as against authors like Duff, that in punishment we are not properly concerned with the inner mental state of the individual who is being punished, but only with what they can be publicly seen to undergo.[29] Alternatively, we might locate an offender's agency at an earlier point – for example their entering of a plea in the criminal process. However this also seems problematic. It seems perverse to see an offender's entering a plea, at a point at which his or her guilt is take to be formally undecided, as embodying an intention to cause an audience to believe that they have done something wrong.[30]

The main problem with Bennett's account is that punishment is something which is imposed by the state on an offender. This seems inconsistent with viewing it as a process in which the offender (or indeed any agent other than the state or those who act on its behalf) express anything at all. If we wish to modify the Simplified Nozickian View in a way that will enable us to solve the problems encountered in Section 5, we will have to consider other possibilities.

8   The recipient of penal communication

In introducing the Simplified Nozickian View I focused (as Nozick himself does) on the idea that punishment expresses a reprobative message to a particular recipient: namely, an offender (or putative offender). However,

---

[29]   Bennett 2008 pp.147–8; cf. Bennett 2006.

[30]   Especially if we want to see it as involving the expression of something else entirely, such as a putative offender accepting of the authority of the court which is trying them (as Duff 2007 suggests).

it is worth noticing that this need not be an essential part of a version of expressivism based on Gricean ideas. Grice requires that for an action to mean something it must be intended to make someone – call them the 'recipient' of the message – believe something, recognize the intention that he should believe something and have as his or her reason the recognition of this intention. However this leaves something underspecified: namely who, exactly the recipient might be.

Nozick portrays punishment in a way which suggests that it is a transaction which essentially only involves two people – a figure who offends, and who is subjected to punishment, and an authority who inflicts this punishment on him or her. If we think of punishment in this way then it is natural to think that the intended recipient of the message which punishment is supposed to deliver must be the individual who is being punished. (Except in pathological cases, the individual or authority inflicting punishment is presumably not attempting to get him or herself to believe that the punished agent has done something wrong.) However, this portrayal seems to leave out something significant, at least where legal punishment is concerned.

In this case it is less obvious that there are only two agents involved. Criminal trials are, in an important sense, public events. They are not public simply in the sense that they deal with matters of public concern. They are also – at least typically – a form of ritual performance which takes place in view of the public. This, then, suggests that if punishment has an expressive function, that function may involve expressing something to someone other than the offender.[31] It may, rather, involve expressing something to the community whose laws the offender has infringed.

It will be helpful to introduce some terminology at this point. Following Uma Narayan, I shall call expressive accounts on which the principal audience of penal communication is the offender 'communicative accounts', and accounts on which the principal audience is society as a whole 'denunciatory accounts'. (Since we are interested in cases of legal punishment, we might substitute the term 'the political community' with 'society'; but it is worth bearing in mind that there might in principle be denunciatory accounts of other forms of punishment.

One might wonder how significant the distinction between communicative and denunciatory accounts really is. After all in many cases of legal punishment, the offender who is punished will be a member of the

---

[31] Duff 2007; Duff et al. 2007.

political community who is doing the punishing. If the message that punishment is supposed to express is supposed to be expressed to the members of the political community, then it will be expressed to the offender, among others. If this is correct then a denunciatory account of punishment will also be a communicative account. Furthermore, and more importantly, denunciatory accounts will be subject to the same kinds of objections, and to the same degree, as communicative accounts.

There are two things to say in response to this point. The first is that although it may be true that in paradigmatic cases of punishment the offender being punished will be a member of the political community that is doing the punishing, this need not always be the case. We generally think that states have a right to punish individuals who commit crimes on their territory, even when they are not citizens of the state in question. So in a case like this, the fact that a message is expressed to the citizens of a state will not entail that is expressed to an offender. To that extent the denunciatory account does not entail the communicative one: they will need to give different accounts of the punishment of non-citizens.

A second point, whose significance will emerge in due course, is that although it is true that the denunciatory account and the communicative account entail that in the paradigmatic case of punishment – that of the punishment of a citizen by a state of which they are a member – a message is expressed to the offender, there is still a significant difference between how we think of the offending citizen as being addressed. On the communicative account he or she is being addressed *qua* offender; on the denunciatory account *qua* citizen. This distinction will play a part in explaining why denunciatory views are not subject to the kinds of problems that I raised for the Simplified Nozickian View.

9   Reconsidering the content of penal communication

We might wonder whether denunciatory accounts will succumb to the problems which I raised for the Simplified Nozickian View in Section 5. It may seem obvious that they will. For we might think that if there is something problematic about the state setting itself up as something which should be regarded as a moral authority by offenders, there is also something problematic about the idea of the state setting itself up as something that should be regarded as a moral authority by members of the political community other than the offender. However, matters are not quite as simple as this suggests.

If an offender has committed a criminal action of a particular type, there is often no need to convey to him or her that he or she has performed an action of that type. Thieves typically know that they have stolen; murderers typically know that they have murdered, and so on. No plausible expressive theory could take it to be a significant part of the function of punishment to communicate to an offender that they have committed such an act. There may be cases where an offender is in genuine doubt as to whether they have committed a criminal act (and other cases where they are in doubt as to which crime they have committed); but it is not clear why the imposition of punitive harsh treatment would be a more effective way of communicating this to them than the deliverance of a clear and authoritative judgment by a properly constituted body.

By contrast it will, in general, be far from pointless to communicate to members of a community that a particular individual has performed a particular kind of action. This is not something which will typically be a matter of common knowledge. So we might wonder whether a denunciatory theorist could take punishment to have the function of expressing the message that an offender has committed a particular kind of crime. A view of this sort would be able to escape the objection put forward in Section 5. In communicating via punishment, the state would not be representing itself as an expert on moral matters but only on the question of what an offender had done, and how to classify it from a legal point of view. There is nothing obviously objectionable about the state representing itself as having this kind of expertise.

However, a denunciatory account of this sort seems obviously unsatisfactory. It seems to make punishment superfluous. For there is something else which expresses the message in question: the act in which an individual who has been tried for a crime is convicted. (Someone might object than an act cannot properly be described as an act of convicting a criminal unless it is intended to be followed by the pronouncing of a sentence and the carrying out of due punishment. But we can imagine a set of judicial institutions which were like ours in their procedures for determining whether an individual had violated a particular norm, but did not involve the pronouncing of sentence. Such an action would have the same expressive role which we are here supposing punishment to have.)

This point does not show that punishment could not have as the whole of its expressive function the communication of a message as to what the offender had done. However, it would raise obvious questions about the extent to which the expressive function, so conceived, could play a significant role in justifying punishment. Given the expense of our punitive institutions, and the fact that they typically involve inflicting on offenders treatments which it would not be permissible to inflict on the in the absence of wrongdoing, some further justification would need to be given which would explain why this particular form of expression should be worthwhile.

This suggests that any plausible denunciatory view will have to be one on which the message expressed in punishment incorporates a reprobative element. Here is a suggestion along these lines: the message expressed by a punishment is that an offender has committed a particular crime, and, in committing that crime, has acted wrongly. This message should be regarded as being decomposable into two parts: the first is that the offender has committed a crime of a particular nature; the second is that in so acting, the offender has acted wrongly. On this account, the content of the communication expressed in punishment goes beyond the communication expressed in the delivery of a conviction. So the institution of punishment is not immediately shown to be superfluous.

It is an important part of this suggestion that the second part of the message expressed by punishment should be not simply that the criminal has acted wrongly; but rather that, in virtue of having acted in a particular way, they have acted wrongly. If the message were simply that an act of a particular type was wrong, the account would be unsatisfactory for a reason very similar to one of the reasons why the Simplified Nozickian View seemed unsatisfactory. We cannot take a punishing authority's act of punishment to be intended to communicate to the political community at large that – say – murder is wrong, because in order to mean that, the punishing authority would have to intend that the recipient of the message come to believe that murder was wrong, and come to believe it through recognizing that the punishing authority intended to communicate that very message. Since it is to be hoped that a large part of the supposed audience of this communication would already believe that murder was wrong, and that this fact would be known by the punishing authority, the punishing authority cannot have the necessary intentions. So it cannot intend to communicate to them that murder is wrong.

By contrast the punishing authority can intend to communicate to members of a political community that in committing murder, the offender has acted wrongly. For, it will presumably not be a matter of general knowledge that a particular offender has committed murder. If so, it will not be a matter of common knowledge that in committing murder they have acted wrongly. So this is something which a punishing authority can intend to communicate.

The objection that punishment is a superfluous message can be reformulated in ways that seem to make trouble for this suggestion. Suppose we take the existence of certain kinds of laws to embody a commitment to the wrongness of some kinds of action. Thus, for example, we take the existence of a prohibition against murder to be a public expression that murder is wrong. Suppose also that convicting someone of murder is a public expression of the claim that that individual has committed murder. Suppose we also think of courts and legislative bodies as speaking on behalf of the political community, where this is conceived of as a kind of collective agent.

Several philosophers have held that if we see a body as a collective agent, then in situations where we take the collective agent to be committed to P and to be committed to Q and P and Q together entail R, we should take the commitment to P and Q to constitute a commitment to R. We might then think that public expression of the claim that murder is wrong, together with a public expression of the claim that a particular individual is a murderer, amounts to a public expression that the individual who has committed murder has done wrong. If so, it is not clear what need there would be for a further act expressing this fact. Punishment would once again turn out to be superfluous.

However, this condition on collective commitment seems too strong. It seems to rule out *a priori* the possibility of collectives holding irrational sets of beliefs. But on the face of it, this does not seem to be impossible: collective agents seem to be as capable of irrationality, and of the particular kind of irrationality which involves failing to draw appropriate conclusions from the things they believe as individuals are. If they can, then this argument for the superfluousness of punishment fails. [32]

10   State, society and the denunciatory view

In Section 5 I argued that the Simplified Nozickian View faced a difficulty, insofar as the reprobative element it incorporates requires the state to present a distorted account of itself to offenders. In Section 9, I argued that in order to avoid making punishment superfluous, a denunciatory

---

[32] This is consistent with holding, along with Davidson 1980, that too much irrationality of this sort might compromise any putative agent's claim to be an agent.

account of punishment needs to incorporate a reprobative account. We might wonder whether the arguments put forward in Section 5 make the account proposed in Section 9 untenable. This issue seems especially pressing since the problem for the Simplified Nozickian View did not arise because of some special feature of the relationship between the state and offenders, but simply because there appeared to be something problematic about the idea of the state claiming moral expertise. The identity of the audience of these pronouncements played no explicit role in the argument.

We can address this question by returning to the question of the relationship between society and the state. If – as I suggested in Section 4 – we think of the state as a kind of collective agent, then it will be natural to ask how that collective agent is related to the individuals who form the society over which that state has authority. Margaret Gilbert has put forward a persuasive answer to this question. She has argued that we should understand the state as being a collective agent which is constituted out of the individuals over whom the state claims authority.[33] This view allows for an interesting answer to questions about the nature of political obligation.

On Gilbert's view, political obligations are the kinds of obligations which we are subject to when we are engaged in any kind of collective activity. On her view, although these obligations have normative force, they are not moral obligations. They are consequences of being committed to collective activity, in the same way that a commitment (such as an intention) to engage in some individual activity may give rise to commitments to engage in parts of that activity. Gilbert's view also allows for an attractive account of the nature of law: law-making activity can be regarded as the activity of forming and entering into collective commitments, and these commitments can be regarded as binding in the same way, and for the same kinds of reasons that collective intentions can be regarded as binding.[34]

If Gilbert's view of the state and of law is viable, then denunciatory theorists have a natural response to the worries we have been considering in the last three sections of this chapter. For on this kind of account, the

---

[33] Gilbert 2006.

[34] Gilbert's account has something in common with what are sometimes described as 'actual consent' theories of political obligation. However, it is not part of her view that one needs to have explicitly consented to become part of a collective body in order to for one to be so, and to have the kinds of obligations that follow from being so: one can, as it were become aware that one is a member of a collective 'in media res'.

reprobative message of punishment goes from the state to its citizens. In other words it will involve a message communicated from the citizens of a state (considered as a collective body) to the citizens of that same state (considered as individuals). In other words it will involve the expression of a judgment made by a collective to the members of that collective. While there may seem something problematic about the state setting itself up as a moral authority over offenders, it is less clear that there must be something problematic about a group of citizens expressing a message to its own members about what they are committed to in virtue of being members of that society.

One might think that there is something problematic about the idea of an agent communicating with itself. We might agree with Wittgenstein that just as there is no such thing as giving oneself a five pound note, there is no such thing as communicating with oneself.[35] We might even think that the impossibility of communicating with oneself follows from the Gricean account of communication put forward in Section 3, since there seems to be something problematically circular about the idea of having the intention to bring oneself to believe something by recognizing one's intention that one believe that very thing. Or we might think that it is superfluous to communicate with oneself. However, the account I have put forward does not involve any agent communicating with itself. It involves a collective agent communicating with a number of individuals which constitute that agent. This does not seem to be as problematic as the idea of an agent communicating with itself.

However, even if we think that it is intelligible to think of a collective body communicating with its members in the way I have been suggesting, we might wonder what purpose such communication could serve. One significant goal is that of expressing a collective commitment to the values that are embodied in the laws. Several authors have argued that there is something incoherent in the idea that society could be committed to certain norms if they never sanctioned those who transgressed against them. Whether or not this is correct, it does seem plausible to claim that one way in which a collective subject might express a commitment to certain norms might be by sanctioning individual members who fail to uphold such commitments in conspicuous ways, such as offending against them.

In Section 6 I argued that we could distinguish between the state's expression of a message to an offender qua citizen and addressing itself to an offender qua offender. We are now in a position to have a clearer

---

[35] Wittgenstein 1949 section 268.

idea of what this distinction is and why we might regard it as significant. Here is one way of understanding the distinction. In addressing an offender as a citizen, a state – conceived of as a body of individuals who have undertaken a joint commitment of a certain sort – seeks to re-iterate to one of the individuals who has undertaken that commitment precisely what the commitment that they have undertaken is. The fact that penal communication involves harsh treatment makes it an especially forceful way of communicating this. But the key point is that it is a commitment that is in some sense a commitment undertaken by the citizen (who happens to be an offender). He is addressed, as it were, as 'one of us', rather than 'one of them'.

This point provides us with a plausible answer to the point about moral authority which I raised in Section 5. There I argued that it was problematic to see punishment as communicating a reprobative message to an offender, because in doing so, the state would be presenting itself as having a kind of authority that it could not be plausibly be seen as having. But the idea that a group might communicate such a message to one of its members does not seem so obviously problematic. We might follow Gilbert in taking that it that in so doing, the state was merely reiterating a commitment to which the offender was already committed. So seen we could not regard the state as involved in undermining the autonomy of the citizen in a morally problematic way.

11 Concluding remarks

The idea that punishment involves communicating with citizens is intended to explain how a denunciatory theory of punishment might be equipped to respond to one particular problem that might be thought to lie in the way of any such account: that of how the state can have the kind of moral authority that this account would suggest. It is not supposed to entail that there are no states in which the inflicting of punishment is problematic in ways that the objection suggests. It may be that there are states which are not appropriately conceived of as collective agents constituted out of the aggregate of their citizens.

The account offered falls short of being an adequate account of the justifiability of punishment in one especially conspicuous way. As we saw in Chapter 1, punishment is typically understood as involving treatment which is in some sense 'harsh'. I argued that although this notion should not be understood the intentional inflicting of suffering on an offender, it should be understood in a way which will entail that punishment will typically cause an offender to suffer. Nothing that has been said in this chapter speaks to the questions of the kinds of means by which the state might be permitted to express reprobative messages; whether it might be permitted to express such messages through the medium of inflicting harsh treatment upon offenders; and whether the function of punishment is one which necessitates inflicting harsh treatment on offenders. We might then wonder, even in the light of everything that has been said in this chapter, whether the expression of a collective commitment to norms need take the form of punishment as that notion is typically understood. I shall address this question in Chapter 4.[36]

---

[36] I am grateful to Lars Vinx for a number of comments on earlier drafts of this chapter, which saved me from several blunders, and forced me to clarify my thinking on a number of issues. He is obviously not responsible for any blunders or unclarities that may remain.

4
Expression, Publicity and Harsh Treatment

1 Introduction

Many philosophers hold that punishment has an expressive dimension.[1] Such philosophers may disagree about the message being expressed by punishment, and the agent doing the expression. As we have seen they may also differ about the audience (if any) to whom the message is expressed. In Chapter 3, I outlined a denunciatory account of punishment, on which the intended recipients of the message which punishment communicates are the members of the society whose laws have been broken and not (or at least not in the first instance) the offender.

In this chapter I shall return to the question of the audience to which the messages which punishment is supposed to express. For I shall argue that denunciatory views are able to give a better response to two important challenges which any version of expressivism faces than other versions of expressivism. The challenges I have in mind arise from two features of punishment which any plausible theory of legal punishment needs to accommodate: the fact that the kind of punishment that our legal systems dispense is in an important sense a public matter and the fact that it involves harsh treatment.

I shall call these challenges the 'harsh treatment challenge' and the 'publicity challenge' respectively. The first has received considerable discussion in the literature on expressive theories of punishment; the second considerably less. I think that this is unfortunate. For careful

---

[1] They include Feinberg 1965 Nozick 1981 Duff 1986, 2001 Falls 1987 Hampton 1988, 1992 Primoratz 1989 Kleinig 1991, von Hirsch 1993, 1999, Metz 2000, 2007 Bennett 2008 and Glasgow (forthcoming).

consideration of the publicity challenge should lead us to favor a version of the expressive theory which has been under-discussed: the view on which punishment has an intended audience, and on which the audience is society at large, rather than – as on the most popular version of that view – the criminal. Furthermore, this view turns out to be better equipped to meet the harsh treatment challenge, and to be so precisely because of the way in which it meets the publicity challenge.

2   Punishment as expressive: audience-dependent and audience-independent views

As we have seen, some expressivists think that what punishment expresses must be expressed to a particular audience. For example, Antony Duff holds that punishment should be intended to communicate a message of disapproval *to a particular offender*.[2] However, one can hold that the message that punishment expresses is one which is expressed to a particular audience, without taking the offender to be that audience. One might instead think of punishment as a communication expressed to the public or society as a whole. This view is suggested both by Hampton, who writes that 'the retributivist...wants the moral truth to be heard'[3] and Primoratz, who writes 'punishment is not like a private letter; it is like a billboard put up on a busy street...it is also meant for the victim of crime *and for the public at large'*.[4] Both Hampton and Primoratz seem to have in mind the possibility that the public or members of society might be an important secondary audience for punishment.[5] But we might also take this to be the primary audience of penal communications.[6]

Call views on which it is essential to the justification of punishment that it express something to an audience 'audience-dependent' versions of expressivism. It will be convenient to have labels for different kinds of audience-dependent views. I shall call views like Duff's, on which communication is addressed primarily to an offender 'communicative' views and views on which it is expressed primarily to society at large

---

[2] Duff 2001; Tasioulas 2006.

[3] Hampton 1988 p. 132.

[4] Primoratz 1989 p. 200 (italics mine).

[5] Though for Primoratz 1989, it is an important secondary audience, since it plays a significant role in explaining why punishment should involve harsh treatment.

[6] As Primoratz 1989 seems, at times to suggest.

'denunciatory views'.[7] As we have seen, there are also views on which both communicative and denunciatory forms of expression play an important role in justifying punishment: we might call such views as 'hybrid views'. We should also notice the possibility of what one might call 'indeterminate views' on which the justification of punishment depends on it communicating to some audience or other rather than to any particular audience.

One might think that the justifiability of punishment does not depend on its expressing something to an audience, but simply on its expressing something *tout court*. I shall call such views 'audience-independent' versions of expressivism.[8] Audience-independent expressivism may seem a somewhat counter-intuitive view. It might, however be motivated on the basis of the idea that there is a close constitutive link of some sort between holding and expressing certain kinds of values.[9] If one holds a view of this sort and takes it to be either valuable or mandatory to hold certain kinds of values, then one might take this fact to play a role in justifying punishment. A justification of this sort may (but need not be) audience-independent.

The view that there is a constitutive link between holding certain kinds of values and expressing them through punishment is well-expressed by John Kleinig, who writes:

> Punishment, I want to claim, is conditionally called for by moral dereliction – as an index of the seriousness of that kind of breach in human relations. It is a measure of the importance that we give to morality in our lives that we deem it appropriate to respond punitively. ... And when moral expectations are violated, we show scant regard for ourselves or for others as the distinctive beings we are if we

---

[7] The terminology originates with Narayan 1993. We might also want to consider the possibility that the relevant audience is the *victim* of the crime. However, an account of punishment on which the justifiability of punishment depended entirely on its expressing something to the victim of crime would be unsatisfactory. Some crimes – for example, speeding on an empty road – do not have a clearly identifiable victim; and some crimes, such as murder, whose victims cannot have their value communicated to them by the punishment of an offender. If we think that speeders and murderers should be punished and that the justifiability of punishment depends on it communicating something to an audience, then the audience in question cannot be a victim.

[8] Audience-independent versions of expressivism have been defended by Metz 2000 and Glasgow (forthcoming). Glasgow suggests that Kleinig 1991 also holds an audience-independent view. See below for my dissent.

[9] Anderson 1993; Metz 2007; Glasgow (forthcoming).

do not act in a negative or critical manner. Indeed, I want to suggest, unless punishment is seen as warranted by such breaches, we fail to accord morality the seriousness it deserves.[10]

Kleinig does not hold an audience-independent view, since he later suggests that

> In imposing on the wrongdoer punitively, we give expression to our condemnation of his conduct, and attempt to bring home to him what he has done.[11]

Thaddeus Metz has suggested the possibility of an audience-independent version of expressivism. He holds that there is a sense of the word 'censure' (though perhaps not the normal speaker's sense of the word) on which to censure someone is to express disapproval of them for a wrong taken to have been done by them, even when this disapproval can be done in a way that involves no audience.[12] He also suggests that the view that the state has a duty to censure injustice 'uniquely matches central intuitions about justice'.[13] These intuitions are that the state has obligations to disavow unjust actions, to affirm the worth of victims, and to treat offenders as responsible. Metz's position seems to leave open the possibility that a state might succeed in fulfilling these duties while censuring in an audience-dependent manner.[14]

3 The publicity challenge

I shall argue that considerations about the public nature of punishment present a *prima facie* difficulty for both audience-independent and communicative versions of expressivism. First, however, I need to address a preliminary worry about the role that considerations of this sort will play in my argument. For we might think that one distinctive

---

[10] Kleinig 1991 p. 410.

[11] Ibid. p. 418. Kleinig adds that 'Sometimes things should be said even if people are impervious to them. That they are said registers the ` importance they have.' But this not, by itself evidence of commitment to an audience-independent view: he might instead hold that it is important that the things which are said are said to the very people who are, as it happens, impervious to them. Kleinig 1991 p. 418.

[12] Metz 2000 p. 496.

[13] Ibid.

[14] Glasgow forthcoming interprets Metz in this way.

and desirable feature of contemporary societies, and one way in which they are superior to pre-modern ones is that in them it is the criminal trial, rather than the process of punishment that is most conspicuously a public matter.[15]

This worry is best addressed by being explicit about the ways in which punishment is a public matter.[16] One has to do with the procedures of the law. Law courts are public buildings; the outcomes of criminal proceedings (and often the proceedings themselves) are a matter of public record, and can be publicly challenged so and on. A second has to do with the outcomes of the criminal law: punishment is a public matter, both in the sense that the imposition of punishments is a matter of public record, but also in the sense that punishments imposed can affect one's status as a member of the public. This is most obvious where punishments involving imprisonment are concerned: in being imprisoned one is deprived of one's liberty, but one is also deprived of the ability to participate in public life. But some forms of punishment can affect other aspects of one's capacity to engage in public life, such as a person's eligibility for certain forms of employment and (in some places) to vote. The first of these senses of publicity seems to entail the second. This point is compatible with an insistence that the ways in which punishment is of necessity carried out under the gaze of the public need not and should not be treated as a reason for taking the purpose of either trial or punishment to be that of humiliating an offender.[17]

Reflection on the public nature of punishment suggests that an audience-independent view might be harder to motivate than we initially supposed. Consider Metz's argument (which I discussed in Section 2) for the claim that the state has a duty to censure offenders. The considerations Metz mentions do not support an audience-independent view.[18] For if the state has the obligations Metz mentions, it seems more plausible that

---

[15] Duff et al. 2007 citing Foucault 1977 on the historical claim.

[16] It is worth distinguishing these from two further respects in which one might take punishment to be a public matter. One concerns the subject matter of criminal law: Duff 2001 has argued that the only kinds of wrong which we should regard as properly falling under the view of the criminal law are what he calls 'public wrongs'; those in which the state legitimately has an interest. A second has to do with the fact that within the setting of the criminal trial – and thus in determining whether punishment is appropriate, and also, on the communicative view, when imposing punishment, a judge (and perhaps also the members of a jury) speak on behalf of the public.

[17] This concern seems to underlie the point which Duff and his co-authors make.

[18] Pace Glasgow (forthcoming).

it has a duty to disavow certain forms of behavior or to affirm the worth of victims to a particular audience – namely, its own citizens – than that it has a duty to engage in audience-independent forms of expression. If the duty could be fulfilled by engaging in audience-independent means of expression, it is hard to see why secret forms of expression would be disqualified from fulfilling it. But it is at best highly counter-intuitive to suppose that a state could satisfy the duty to disavow the behavior of wrongdoers by issuing secret denunciations of wrongdoing.

The publicity of punishment raises further problems for audience-independent expressivism. On an audience-independent view the justification of punishment depends on its being a manifestation of an emotion which is an appropriate response to a particular kind of wrongdoing. It is not essential to its being such a manifestation that it should be public. Furthermore punishments that are public, in the sense which I have been considering here will in many cases make offenders liable to feel shame. Shame is in general a painful emotion. There seems no reason from an audience-independent expressivist point of view to prefer forms of expression which bring shame on an offender over ones which do not. And there may be reasons for avoiding such forms of punishment: they may stigmatize offenders, making it more difficult for them to be re-integrated into society, and increase their chances of re-offending.

The publicity of punishment also raises problems for communicative theorists such as Duff. Duff thinks we should understand punishment as a form of communication which is addressed to an offender in the hope of prompting remorse and reconciliation. It is not clear why a communication of this sort needs to be public: why, that is, it needs to be overheard – as it were – by individuals to whom it is not directly addressed. A communicative theorist might take the experience of shame and stigmatization to play a significant role in conveying the message which such a theorist thinks should be conveyed by punishment. However Duff has distanced himself from an account of punishment on which the shaming of offenders plays a significant role, and at least some of the literature on the damaging effects of shame and stigmatization suggest that he is right to do so.[19]

Denunciatory versions of expressivism can easily account for the public nature of punishment. Punishment can only communicate something to a given audience if the audience is able to become aware of it. Punishment needs to be a public matter in the second of the senses

---

[19] For a good overview see Braithwaite 2000.

I have distinguished for this to be possible.[20] Consider Primoratz's comparison between punishment and a public billboard. There is no point in putting up a billboard that no-one can see.

Do the points that I have made about shame and stigmatization pose a problem for the denunciatory view as well as for communicative and audience-dependent views? The denunciatory view does not claim that shame and stigmatization are not harmful. So advocates of a denunciatory view do have something to worry about here. However, the problem they face is rather different from the problem faced by advocates of communicative and audience-dependent views. On the denunciatory view, the harms of shame and stigmatization arise from aspects of punishment which play a central role in the justification of punishment. We must therefore ask whether we are justified in imposing these harms in order to achieve the ends which we take punishment to aim at. In other words, we are faced with a version of the 'harsh treatment challenge'. I shall discuss this challenge in Sections 5–8 below.

By contrast, on the communicative and audience-dependent views, the harms of shaming and stigmatization seem to arise out of features of punishment which do not play an essential part in justifying the practice. We therefore need to explain why we would be justified in imposing these harms when we engage in a practice which is justified by the kinds of considerations an advocate of a communicative or audience-independent view would take to be significant.

4 Responding to the publicity challenge

I have argued that attention to the public nature of punishment provides us with reasons for preferring denunciatory versions of expressivism to audience-independent and communicative versions. However, these reasons will be undermined if advocates of those views can provide alternative, equally good accounts of why punishment should be a public matter. I shall consider three. One is that there are pragmatic grounds for thinking that punishment should be public in this sense. It may simply be cheaper, or more effective. A second is that making punishment public in this sense protects against certain kinds of abuse. A third

---

[20] Bennett 2008 has emphasized the public nature of punishment in arguing for his version of expressivism. On Bennett's view, punishment is a way for offenders to make a publicly dramatized expression of remorse. However, we might be impressed by the public nature of punishment without accepting Bennett's claim that we should be concerned with expression on the part of the offender rather than on the part of state.

is that the publicity of punishment is best accounted for by considerations of the nature of the trial. If any of these considerations provide a plausible explanation for the publicity of punishment, then the account I am putting forward fails.

If communicative and audience-dependent theories were neutral on the question of whether punishment should be public, the fact that punishment might be cheaper or more effective if it is public might provide an adequate justification of the publicity of punishment. In Section 3, I argued that these theories are not neutral on this issue: on both views considerations about shame and stigmatization constitute reasons why punishment should not be public. Considerations of cost and effectiveness would have to outweigh these reasons. Furthermore these considerations would have to be ones which justified imposing harms on convicted offenders which went beyond those that were required by the communicative and expressive goals of punishment. As such they would, require an advocate of one of these two views to be able to give a response to the problem of harsh treatment. As we shall see in Sections 4–6 below, we should be skeptical about whether they can.

The suggestion that punishment needs to be a public matter in order to prevent abuse seems more promising. Since the prevention of abuse is something that protects convicted offenders rather than harming them, it does not seem to raise the same sorts of problems as a justification based on considerations of effectiveness or cost. However, in practice the public nature of punishment does not seem to be a particularly effective way of preventing abuse of convicted offenders: rates of such abuse vary from penal system to another, and can be high even when punishment is a public matter. Furthermore, even if penal systems require some form of public scrutiny in order to prevent abuse, they do not require that punishment be a public matter in the sense that I have been concerned with here. They do not require, in other words, that the fact of a particular individual's punishment be a matter of public record, or that punishment affect an offender's civic status.

The public nature of punishment might be thought to follow from a normative theory of the trial. Antony Duff and his co-authors have argued for an account of the trial on which trials must be public.[21] Their account explores how the publicity of the trial illuminates and justifies features of criminal law which we might otherwise struggle to explain, such as the presumption of innocence, the high burden of proof that

---

[21] Duff et al. 2007.

is required in criminal trials, and the right to silence on the part of the accused. If the public nature of punishment is simply a consequence of the public nature of the trial, this might provide a justification of the publicity of punishment which would be as good as the justification given on behalf of the denunciatory account earlier in Section 2. If so, the public nature of punishment will not constitute a reason for preferring denunciatory theories to other versions of expressivism.

However, an account like this could only provide a justification of public punishment if it included an explanation of why trials should be public in this sense. This might seem easy to provide. There are certain respects in which criminal trials must be public. For example it is natural to see judges and perhaps also members of criminal juries speaking, when they do so from within their officially defined roles, on behalf of the public. Furthermore Duff and Tadros have both defended the view that publicity must be invoked in order to explain which wrongs are properly the business of the criminal law: they are on this view public wrongs in the sense of being wrongs which are properly the concern of the public.[22]

However caution is needed here.[23] As I noted earlier, publicity is a multi-faceted word and a process which is public in one of these senses need not necessarily be public in any of the others. In particular it does not follow from the fact that an action is carried out on behalf of the public, and in which the public has some legitimate interest, must be carried out in view of the public. To think otherwise is to offer a quick and implausible argument against a government engaging in any activity in secret whatsoever. This conclusion seems too strong: there are surely activities carried out on behalf of the public and in the interests of the public which may legitimately be carried out in secret.

5 The harsh treatment problem

In Sections 3 and 4 I argued that for the denunciatory theorist of punishment, though not for the audience-independent expressivist or the communicative theorist, the Publicity Challenge can be seen as a version of the Harsh Treatment challenge. I shall now argue that unlike the communicative and audience-independent expressivist, the

---

[22] Duff 2001; Tadros 2005. See also Duff 2007 for the idea that in a criminal trial a defendant is called upon to answer for their actions *to* the public.

[23] Duff 2001; Tadros 2005.

denunciatory theorist has a convincing response to the Harsh Treatment Challenge.

In this section I shall set out the Harsh Treatment Challenge. In Section 6, I shall show that the audience-independent expressivist cannot meet it; and in Section 7 I shall show that the communicative theorist cannot meet it either. Along the way, I shall address an objection to communicative views which has been raised by Joshua Glasgow, which arises from a consideration of the possibility of unreceptive offenders. Doing so will help us to see that it is the harsh treatment problem rather than the problem of unreceptive offenders which presents the biggest obstacle to the communicative view, and also prepare the ground for responding to an objection that Glasgow has leveled against the denunciatory view and which is modeled on the unreceptive offender problem.

Punishing someone typically involves treating them in ways which they find unpleasant, and in which we would not normally be permitted to treat them, in the absence of their consent, outside of a punitive context. In imprisoning people, we deprive them of their liberty: this may be found burdensome by itself; or it may be found burdensome insofar as it deprives an individual of the opportunity to pursue their interests. If a monetary fine is imposed on someone, we expect it to have a negative effect on their well-being. And when people are sentenced to community service, the tasks they are assigned are often intended to be deliberately tedious, and on some occasions a source of shame. I leave on one side forms of punishment which involve the deliberate infliction of physical pain or death: here the point is obvious.

Some authors think that punishment must involve an intention to cause an offender to suffer.[24] I argued in Chapter 2 that this is incorrect. On the account of punishment (and in particular of harsh treatment) that I defended there, we will not have failed to punish someone if we impose on them a fine which imposes no financial hardship (though we may have failed to punish them effectively). However I also argued that punishment inflicts suffering in a manner that is non-accidental: if a (supposed) sanction which never caused suffering to anyone were imposed on an individual, it would be difficult to understand why we should regard it as a form of punishment.

The fact that punishment typically involves treating someone harshly appears to raise a problem for expressivists. We normally think that the fact that a certain practice can be expected to cause suffering is a reason against engaging in it. It is not necessarily a conclusive reason: there

---

[24] Hanna 2008; Boonin 2008.

may be occasions on which we can only achieve an important goal at the cost of inflicting suffering on someone. Under such circumstances, we may be justified in doing something that we expect will impose suffering on someone.[25] Nevertheless it seems plausible that in most cases the fact that a practice will predictably cause someone to suffer is at least a contributory reason against engaging in it. If we can find a way of achieving the same goals in ways that do not cause suffering, or cause it to a lesser degree, then these means are, to that extent, preferable.

Someone who thinks that our penal institutions are justified in virtue of their expressive features needs to do one of two things. They must either show that there are no ways of treating offenders that have the same the same expressive features as punishment does, but which do not predictably cause this level of suffering; or explain why the sorts of reasons we have for not engaging in practices which cause suffering when there alternative means to the same goals are either inapplicable, or over-ruled by other considerations.

6   Responding to the harsh treatment problem: audience-independent views

Advocates of audience-dependent versions of expressivism often appeal to the way in which the harsh treatment that punishment affects an audience in order to account for its role in punishment. Kleinig, advocating a communicative version of expressivism, puts the point thus:

> For the most part our sensitivities are too dull, our hypocrisy too common, for mere face-to-face blaming to make its point... Unless we see or experience some form of hard treatment, we are likely to remain anaesthetized to the significance of our actions. ... Hard treatment may register where words fail.[26]

Meanwhile Primoratz, appealing to a more denunciation-oriented version of expressivism, suggests that if punishment did not involve some form of harsh treatment, then the victim of the crime and... the public at large. ... would surely see purely verbal condemnation of crime, however public and solemn, as half-hearted and unconvincing. The state would be seen as desisting from activating its apparatus of force and coercion, which is surely one of its essential, defining features.[27]

---

[25] See Tadros 2011 for a detailed exploration of the issues here.
[26] Kleinig 1991 p. 417.
[27] Primoratz 1989 p. 200.

Arguments based on considerations about the conditions which are necessary for the effective communication of a message to an audience are clearly not available to advocates of an audience-independent version of expressivism.

We might suppose that advocates of audience-independent versions of expressivism will find it easier to solve the problem of harsh treatment than advocates of audience-dependent views. For if the justification of punishment depends on its expressing a message to a particular audience, then the possibility of expressing that message in other ways which do not involve harsh treatment might undermine that justification.[28] For example, there might be ways of affirming the value of victims; of communicating with offenders in a way that encourages them to experience regret and remorse; and so on, which do not involve harsh treatment. If there are, then the high moral and practical costs involved in punishing offenders might give us a strong reason for preferring those measures.[29] Audience-independent versions of expressivism seem to avoid objections of this sort. If the justifiability of punishment turns on its being a way of expressing certain kinds of attitude, then the possibility of achieving the (independently specifiable) effects of punishment by some other means will be irrelevant.[30]

This argument for preferring audience-independent versions of expressivism to audience-dependent versions is unpersuasive. It would only be plausible if we thought that an advocate of an audience-dependent view must think of the justificatory role of punishment's being directed at an audience in a particular way: namely via a consideration of the effects of the punishment on its audience. However, this is not the only possibility. Sometimes, though not always, the fact that a certain form of action is expressive in a certain way might require it to be aimed at a particular audience.

Consider two different kinds of case. Sighing might be a way in which I express my boredom with a book I am reading, even if I take myself to be alone and out of earshot of anyone else. By contrast it may be essential to a sigh's being a sigh of resentment or impatience that it is directed to some audience. This can be true even if it is also true that a sigh might

---

[28] Hanna 2008, who depends here on a conception of harshness which I contest in Chapter 1 (cf. footnote 30).

[29] Tadros 2011 chapter 5.

[30] This isn't to rule out the possibility of other closely-related kinds of objection: the possibility of alternative forms of expression; the difficulty of justifying high-cost forms of expression and so on.

succeed in expressing resentment or impatience if the audience at whom it is directed fails to notice it. If punishment is expressive in a way that is analogous to the way in which a sigh can express resentment rather than the way in which a sigh might express boredom, then the existence of an audience for punishment can be relevant to the justification of punishment in ways that do not involve the punishment's having any particular effect on the audience. It can be relevant to determining what it is that punishment expresses or whether it expresses anything at all.

The problem of harsh treatment arises because the fact that a certain practice can be expected to cause suffering seems to provide us with a reason – albeit not a conclusive reason – against engaging in it. Someone who adopts an audience-independent version of expressivism will think there are also reasons in favor of engaging this practice. So something more needs to be said for the objection to bite. What makes the harsh treatment problem bite for advocates of audience-independent expressivism is the apparent possibility of finding alternative ways of expressing the emotions which we currently express via punishment.[31]

This line of argument is more often gestured at than developed in detail. It should be scrutinized carefully. Notice first that the mere logical possibility of forms of expression which differ from our own is of little or no interest to us here. As Joshua Glasgow has emphasized, the forms of expression by which we might express certain values are not infinitely malleable. What can be said with flowers cannot be said with weeds, or with weevils.[32] Insofar as we are interested in responses to wrongdoing that it might, at least in principle, make sense for us to implement, we need to concentrate on forms of expressive response to wrongdoing which are possible for us.

Our expressive possibilities seem to be constrained in a number of ways. For my purposes, it will be helpful to distinguish between two aspects of expressive behavior which we might call natural expressions and cultural elaborations. By natural expressions of emotion I mean such things as trembling as an expression of fear, shouting as an expression of anger, and crying of grief. These forms of expression seem to have some physiological basis; they are cross-culturally shared; and they often involve some involuntary element.[33] When we think of emotions being expressed in behavior, we often have in mind natural expressions

---

[31] As a number of authors, starting with Feinberg 1965, have noted.

[32] Glasgow (forthcoming).

[33] This is not to say that they are never subject to voluntary control. For further elaboration see Griffiths 1997.

of this sort. However, there are other forms of expression that are not like this, but which seem to involve elaborating on the natural expression of emotions in a symbolic manner, in ways which can vary dramatically from culture to culture. Mourning provides a good example here: although mourning rituals vary radically from culture to culture, many of them can be seen as a dramatic elaboration of some of the natural expressions of the emotion of grief.[34]

This distinction between different aspects of emotional expression gives rise to two ways in which the expression of emotions might be constrained. It may be constrained by features of our underlying nature, or by features of the symbolic vocabulary which enable us to elaborate on it. So for example, in the case of an expression of love, the reason we cannot (normally) say it with weevils may be due to the fact that weevils elicit disgust – a straightforwardly physiological matter; whereas the reason we cannot say it with weeds has more to do with culturally variable considerations as to which forms of flowering plant are an appropriate gift to a lover.

How should the audience-independent expressivist think of punishment? It may seem tempting to regard it as the natural expression of an emotion such as resentment at wrongdoing or what Glasgow calls 'punitive hostility'. If so, we would have good reason to regard it as being significantly constrained. For it is plausible that our natural forms of emotional response are constrained by features which are not entirely under our individual or collective control.

Nevertheless, this view seems untenable. While we might think that the natural expression of whichever emotion is expressed by punishment involves harming an offender or a perceived offender, it seems implausible that the elaborate system of social institutions which embody the mechanisms of legal punishment stands to punitive hostility in the way which crying stands to grief. Here we seem to be in the realm of dramatic elaborations of natural responses. As a result there seems to be much more scope for shaping our responses (as there is with mourning).

This is not to deny that dramatic elaborations of our natural responses are also constrained in certain ways. However many of these constraints seem to depend on the ways in which we could naturally expect them to be understood by certain audiences given certain background knowledge – what we might call their social significance. An advocate of audience-independent expressivism seems unable to appeal to this kind of

---

[34] My thinking has been influenced by unpublished work by Christopher Bennett, with whom I disagree substantially on this topic (Bennett forthcoming).

constraint. If a form of expression is not aimed at an audience, it is hard to understand how the way in which an audience might understand it should constrain the form which it should take.

Someone might suggest that the existence of biological constraints on the natural expression of punitive hostility places further constraints on the ways in which it could be dramatically elaborated on. However, it does not follow that these elaborations must take the form of harsh treatment. For we have ways of expressing punitive hostility which do not seem to involve inflicting harsh treatment on individuals. One can do so, for example, by treating their images in certain kinds of ways: burning in them in effigy, spitting on photographs, destroying physical representations and so on. None of these seem to involve harsh treatment. If they do not, they do not constitute punishment. Nevertheless, it seems as though they could serve the expressive goals which the audience-independent expressivist takes to justify punishment. So we do not have a justification of punishment on audience-independent expressivist lines.[35]

7   Responding to the harsh treatment problem II: communicative views

In Section 5, I introduced the Harsh Treatment Problem as the problem of explaining how it can be justifiable to treat people in ways which they can be expected to find burdensome. This formulation pre-empts a possible response to the Harsh Treatment Problem on the part of the communicative theorist. For a communicative theorist might argue, as I did in Chapter 2, that in punishing someone we need not intend that they suffer.[36] If so, they need not be committed to thinking that communicative goals must somehow make it legitimate to intend to inflict suffering.[37]

Communicative theorists cannot escape the formulation of the Harsh Treatment Problem which I have offered quite so easily. For communicative theorists, such as Duff, are committed to a view on which it must be at least predictable that punishment will involve suffering on the part

---

[35] One might think that these are, in fact, forms of harsh treatment, and thus of punishment. It would remain true that the audience-independent expressivist was unable to justify many of the specific forms we typically take to be acceptable forms of punishment, such as deprivation of liberty, monetary fines, and so forth.

[36] See also Wringe 2013.

[37] As, for example, Sayre-McCord 2001 supposes.

of offenders.[38] For Duff holds that punishment is to be justified by its communicating a message to an offender that is intended to make the offender experience remorse, an experience which he takes to be necessarily painful.[39]

Joshua Glasgow has argued that Duff's view has difficulties with what one might call 'unreceptive offenders'.[40] He notes that the plausibility of a communicative view of punishment depends on the medium by which the messages involved in punishment are communicated and the audience to whom they are communicated being well-suited to one another. As he points out, one cannot communicate to an audience that is incapable of grasping the message: one cannot communicate with someone who has no ability to hear over the telephone; with non-Braille readers by means of messages in Braille; with monoglot Anglophones via messages in Chinese, and so on. Call such audiences 'unreceptive'. Glasgow suggests that many of the intended audiences of punishment are, in this sense, unreceptive; they are unable to grasp the message which, on Duff's view, punishment is intended to communicate.[41]

Glasgow intends us to distinguish between offenders who are unreceptive and those who are merely unrepentant. Consider Barry, who rejects the law criminalizing the offense for which he has been committed on principled grounds. Barry understands that a certain kind of punishment has been inflicted with the aim of inducing remorse in him. However he has reflected on whether remorse is called for and decided that it is not. He is unrepentant, but capable of repenting. It is generally accepted (and Glasgow agrees) that offenders like Barry do not present a serious challenge to Duff's view.[42] For Duff holds that although punishment must involve trying to make an offender experience remorse and regret, it is not essential that it succeeds in doing so. Since we can try to make the unrepentant repent, Barry presents no threat to Duff's view.

Contrast Barry with Tarquin, who is simply incapable of grasping (what Duff takes to be) the purpose of a punishment imposed on him. Tarquin sees the infliction of harsh treatment on him as nothing more than society's manifestation of its hostility towards him. He is not merely unrepentant but unreceptive. Glasgow takes Tarquin to present a more serious challenge to Duff's view than Barry. Is he correct? It is hard

---

[38] Duff 2001.
[39] Ibid.
[40] Glasgow (forthcoming).
[41] Ibid.
[42] Tasioulas 2006.

to see why: we can attempt to make Tarquin feel remorse, even if we are destined to fail. Glasgow might object that if we know that this attempt is bound to fail, we cannot intelligibly try to do so. If so, the most we have is an objection to the punishment of offenders who are known to be unreceptive, but not to the punishment of all unreceptive offenders.

Are there offenders whom we can know to be unreceptive to be? Perhaps. But it is not clear that they present a problem for Duff's view. Some offenders who fall into this category may simply be people that it would be inappropriate to punish on any view. Consider Homer, who suffers from cognitive and emotional impairments so great that he is simply incapable of appreciating that an action he has performed is wrong. Homer may be unreceptive; if so we might think that standard justifications of punishment are simply inapplicable to offenders like him: he simply should not be punished. However, the possibility of offenders like Homer does not give us reason to object to the punishment of offenders who are not impaired in the way Homer is.

This response may seem to be satisfactory only if we take offenders whom we can know unreceptive unusual or marginal cases. Glasgow insists that the question of whether or not this is so in a given society is an empirical one. A defender of the communicative view might hold that punishment can only be properly justified in societies where we have good reason to think that most offenders are not unreceptive. Glasgow might reply that that even if we cannot know of a given offender that they are unreceptive, we can know that many of the offenders whom we punish will be. However, even if this is true, it does not help Glasgow. If I do not know, of a given offender, that they are unreceptive, then there is no logical bar to my attempting to make them feel remorse.

Glasgow thinks it would be unsatisfactory to concede that we cannot justify the punishment of unreceptive offenders on the grounds that acknowledging this would run the risk of creating perverse incentives for offenders. If we cannot justify punishing unreceptive offenders, then, he claims, offenders have an incentive to become unreceptive. If such offenders are likely to be worse citizens than their receptive counterparts, punishment will be counterproductive. I have argued that we need only concede the unjustifiability of offenders who are known to be unreceptive. Should we agree that this concession creates perverse incentives?

Not necessarily. The costs of making oneself into such an offender may outweigh the gains. Furthermore, even if we can identify unreceptive offenders, there may be good reasons for an advocate of a communicative view to think that we should avoid shaping our institutions in ways which allow unreceptive offenders to go unpunished. For example we might think that because punishments should express to a receptive offender how seriously they should take transgressions of a particular type, it is essential to the viability of a communicative theory of punishment that the level of punishment be proportionate to the seriousness of an offense. By punishing someone more or less severely on grounds that have to do only with features of the offender and not with features of the seriousness of the offense, we would violate this constraint. If so, then advocates of communicative theories will not support institutions that give rise to perverse incentives to become unreceptive.[43]

Some authors[44] take Duff's response to the problem of harsh treatment to be that remorse or regret offers a means by which an offender may reintegrate themselves into a community, that this is a valuable goal, and that since remorse is an emotion which is necessarily expressed as painful, we have a justification for treating people in ways that they find painful. It is not clear that this response could succeed. Sayre-McCord and Hanna point out that there may be routes to the valuable goal of re-integration that do not involve the painful emotion of remorse, and Christopher Bennett has suggested that even if it might provide a justification for punishment in some kinds of community, it cannot reasonably be taken to provide a justification for punishment within the context of a liberal state, since liberal states should not be concerned with instilling valuable mental states into fully-grown citizens.[45] Igor Primoratz has suggested that taken on its own as a justification for harsh treatment in punishment, it appears to involve an undue degree of solicitude for the fate of an offender in a situation where we might expect the fate of the victim of crime to be of greater significance, and Victor Tadros has argued that even if we take the goal of inducing remorse to be a valuable one, this may not be enough to justify devoting the level of resources that we currently invest in our penal system to achieving it.[46]

The defense of the communicative view being considered here seems inadequate for reasons which are independent of these arguments. Even if it is acceptable for state institutions to inflict on offenders treatment

---

[43] Glasgow suggests that this strategy may involve treating unreceptive offenders as a means. It's not clear to me that this is true, and in the light of Tadros 2011 the point can no longer be regarded as a knock-down argument.

[44] For example Hanna 2008.

[45] Sayre-McCord 2001; Hanna 2008; Bennett 2008.

[46] Primoratz 1989; Tadros 2011.

that causes remorse, it does not follow that it is permissible for the state to cause an offender the other kinds of suffering which our institutions of punishment predictably and reliably produce. Someone who is deprived of their liberty may thereby be led to reflect on their actions and to experience remorse. But the isolation from family, friends or their usual environment which prison entails, and the humiliations involved in living under the kinds of regimes of surveillance that even the most humane forms of confinement might be expected to entail, will lead them to suffer in ways that seem to be independent of their suffering remorse.

Might a communicative theorist appeal to considerations of effectiveness in communication to justify the kinds of harsh treatment that punishment typically involves? They might argue either that communication expressed via harsh treatment is more likely to bring about remorse or that in many cases it is the only way to bring about remorse. However, neither line of argument seems plausible. First, consider the claim that expression via harsh treatment is a more effective way of leading prisoners to feel remorse than communicative condemnation that is not so accompanied. This cannot, by itself constitute a justification of the harsh treatment involved in punishment. It might do so if we thought there was some kind of obligation to adopt the most effective means to inducing remorse. But this is highly implausible. If it is impermissible to treat people in a certain way, then we are obliged to adopt a less effective means, and if it is permissible but highly costly to do so, we might plausibly adopt a less costly means.

Suppose we claim that we are under an obligation to try to make offenders feel remorse and that communication via harsh treatment is the only way of doing so. Some of the considerations which arose in our discussion of unreceptive offenders seem relevant here. We can try to make offenders feel remorse even if we are destined to fail. Of course, we cannot try to do what we know to be impossible. So, if we were in a position to know, of some offenders, that nothing other than harsh treatment could make them feel remorse, we might perhaps be justified in imposing such treatment on them. However, this line of argument will drastically restrict the range of offenders whom we are justified in inflicting harsh treatment on. For most people seem to be unpredictable enough for us to be unsure as to what kinds of treatment might make them feel remorse. Furthermore, the literature on restorative justice suggests that in many cases, engagement with the victims of crime will be more effective in bringing about remorse than standard forms of harsh treatment.[47]

---

[47] Braithwaite 2000.

8 Responding to the harsh treatment challenge III: denunciatory views

In Section 5 I suggested that an expressivist theorist of punishment might argue that harsh treatment was necessary for punishment to achieve its expressive goals. In Section 6, I suggested that an advocate of an audience-independent version of expressivism could not appeal to this argument. In Section 7 I argued that an advocate of a communicative version of expressivism could not do so either. I shall now argue that an advocate of a denunciatory account can do so.

On the Denunciatory View, the idea that harsh treatment is a necessary condition for the effective communication of the message that punishment is supposed to carry to its intended audience is a natural development of a response to the 'Publicity Challenge'. Just as the denunciatory theorist can hold that punishment must be public in order to communicate with its intended audience (since if it is not known to them it cannot communicate anything to them), they can hold that it must involve harsh treatment in order to be taken seriously by that same audience.

A denunciatory theorist should hold that punishment is necessary to communicate to its members that certain norms are accepted, and are to be accepted, in a society. Tadros has argued that expressivists need to explain how the good involved in the kind of expression that punishment involves can justify the costs that punishment involves.[48] Since it may turn out that if the denunciatory theory is correct, we ought to devote fewer resources to punishment than we currently do; the challenge here is to establish that some kind of system of punishment is justifiable, not to justify the particular forms our punitive systems have taken. On the denunciatory view, some enforcement is required in order to demonstrate to the members of a given society that certain norms are the norms of that society.

This already meets Tadros' challenge. But notice also that Tadros holds that the costs involved in punishment can be justified on grounds of deterrence (and that deterrent-based justifications of punishment need not involve impermissibly treating people as means). A denunciatory theorist should hold that the purpose of punishment is not to deter crime but to make it clear that certain norms are to be taken as norms. The goal of establishing that people knowing that certain norms are in force is logically prior to the goal of enforcing those norms. If we can

---

[48] Tadros 2011.

justify the costs involved in punishment by reference to the first goal, then we can also justify them by reference to the second goal.

Duff has suggested that the denunciatory view is objectionable insofar as it treats offenders merely as a means. He holds that on a communicative view, inflicting harsh treatment on an offender does not involve impermissibly treating them as a means because the point of treating them in that way is to express a message to them. The denunciatory theorist seems to have a problem here. On the denunciatory view, the message that punishment expresses is addressed to the members of the society whose laws have been transgressed rather than to the transgressor. However the denunciatory theorist is in fact no worse off than the communicative theorist here. For in paradigmatic cases of punishment, the offender is a member of the society whose laws have been transgressed. Insofar as a message is being expressed to members of that society, it is being expressed to him or her as well. If the advocate of the communicative view can appeal to this fact in order to explain why the use of harsh treatment to communicate with an offender does not involve impermissibly treating the offender as a means, so too can the advocate of the denunciatory view.

Is the denunciatory view vulnerable to a version of Glasgow's 'unreceptive audience' objection discussed in Section 7? Glasgow thinks so: he invokes the possibility of a 'battleground' society, in which individuals do not take punishments to be expressive of society's denunciation of the respective crimes. His discussion of the topic is brief (a single footnote), and it is not clear exactly what he has in mind here. Presumably the idea is one of a society whose members are either so inured to crime that they simply ignore the fact that individuals are being punished, or perhaps it is one of a society whose members are justified in being sufficiently cynical about the institutions of law-enforcement that they take punishments inflicted on offenders to express nothing beyond those institutions' power to harm and humiliate.

The putative possibility of a battleground society does not undermine the plausibility of a denunciatory view. I have already argued that considerations concerning unreceptive offenders are relatively powerless against communicative views. They should seem even less powerful against denunciatory views. For, as deployed against a denunciatory view of punishment, the strongest form of the argument would require it to be the case that every member of the audience to whom the denunciatory message of punishment was expressed should be incapable of understanding the denunciatory role of punishment, and that those who were administering punishment should be in a position to know that this was the case. It seems hard to construct a plausible scenario in which this is likely to be true. And even if we can imagine such a society, it is open to the denunciatory theorist to concede that in such a society, punishment would not be justifiable (or perhaps that it would not be justifiable in the ways that it is in less dysfunctional societies.) In conceding this, they would not be conceding much of either practical or philosophical significance.

9 Conclusion

The question of whether expressivists can justify the harsh treatment that punishment involves has played a central role in discussions of expressive theories of punishment, ever since Feinberg made the view prominent. If the arguments of this chapter are correct, much of that discussion might more profitably have focused on a different feature of punishment, namely its publicity. A refocusing of this sort more quickly reveals which form of expressivism is most plausible – namely a denunciatory view – and makes clear the resources that an expressivist can appeal to in defending this view. Denunciatory versions of expressivism can meet both the Publicity Challenge and the Harsh Treatment Challenge. Other forms of expressivism can meet neither.

Part II
Non-Paradigmatic Punishments

5
Perp Walks as Punishment

1 Introduction

In Part I of this book, I argued in favor of a denunciatory version of an expressive conception of punishment. On an account of this sort, it is essential to any way of treating an offender counting as punishment rather than something else that it should be aimed at communicating a message to members of the political community that is doing the punishing. The fact that punishment has a expressive role is relevant to the justification of punishment: as we saw in Chapter 2, it undermines one kind of argument for thinking that punishment can never be justified. Furthermore, the particular kind of expressive role that punishment has is also relevant to its justification: as we saw in Chapter 4, it is only in the light of the denunciatory function of punishment that we can explain how responses to wrongdoing which involve either publicity or harsh treatment can be justified. However, the account of punishment that I gave in Part I was limited in one very important respect: it dealt only with what I call 'paradigmatic' cases of punishment – in other words, cases where an individual is punished by members of a political community for offenses for which he or she has already been found guilty.

There are many examples of punishment – indeed of putatively justified legal punishment – which do not fit this paradigm. Here are some that seem worth considering (and which I shall deal with during the course of Part II this book): the punishment of corporate entities by states in which they operate; the punishment of individuals convicted of war crimes by international tribunals; and the – under present circumstances, purely hypothetical – punishment of states for breaches of international law. A less obvious non-paradigmatic case that I shall deal with in some detail this chapter is the officially non-punitive treatment of putative offenders before trial: I shall argue that on the conception of punishment I outlined in Part I, we have good reasons to think that this is, in fact, a form of punishment, and that it is objectionable for precisely that reason.

Philosophers of punishment tend to say less about non-paradigmatic cases of punishment than they do about paradigmatic cases of punishment. To my mind, this is a significant shortcoming for two reasons. The first is that philosophers often claim to be engaged in a work of conceptual clarification; and part of the point of such conceptual clarification is supposed to be that it illuminates our understanding of cases that stand on, or near to, the boundary. Such cases often give rise to legitimate philosophical puzzlement. So it seems to be a legitimate test of a philosophical account of punishment that we should test it against non-paradigmatic instances of punishment and see whether it does in fact provide any kind of intellectual illumination.

However, there is a further reason not purely internal to philosophy that arises in non-paradigmatic instances of punishment. This is that some of the legitimate puzzlement we feel about non-paradigmatic instances of punishment relates to questions about the justification of such cases of punishment. Such questions arise here just as often, and with just as much force as they do in paradigmatic cases. Indeed, they sometimes arise with more urgency: while there is little chance that the institution of punishment might be abolished on the basis of philosophical arguments to the effect that it is unjustified; it does seem possible that certain classes of case of non-paradigmatic punishment might be abolished altogether on the basis of philosophical arguments. A philosophical account of punishment which ignores such issues – as many do – seems to be shirking a task which we might reasonably expect philosophers to undertake.

2   Perp walks

When Dominique Strauss-Kahn, then head of the International Monetary Fund (IMF), and widely thought to be a leading contender in the forthcoming French presidential elections, was arrested on charges of sexual assault arising from events that were alleged to have occurred during his stay in an up-market hotel in New York, a sizeable portion of French public opinion was outraged.[1] They were outraged not by the possibility

---

[1] Baker and Erlanger 2011.

that the allegations were true, and that a powerful, well-connected and widely-admired politician had assaulted an immigrant hotel worker, nor by the widely-reported suspicion that the accused had a well-known history of similar behavior to which members of the French political and journalistic elite had turned a blind eye; but rather by the way in which the accused had been treated by the American authorities.[2]

Subsequent events – including the dropping of charges by the New York Police Department(NYPD), and the surfacing of other allegations of sexual misconduct – make it difficult to sympathize with those who saw Strauss-Kahn as a victim; and much of what his defenders had to say, including the suggestion that the whole affair was a conspiracy aimed at removing a French left-winger from his post at the IMF with the aim of replacing him with someone more congenial to American financial interests, and more or less explicit suggestions from the likes of Bernard-Henri Levy that it was beneath the dignity of an important public figure to be treated by the authorities as just another accused individual, evoked distaste at the time, and continue to evoke it in retrospect. To a large extent such distaste seems reasonable and healthy.[3]

Nevertheless, those who defended Strauss-Kahn were correct in one relatively minor respect. The parading of Strauss-Kahn before the press, in handcuffs, did constitute a form of punishment. For such a display to take place when Strauss-Kahn was merely accused, and had not yet stood trial, let alone been found guilty, contravened the principle that criminal punishments should only be administered after a fair trial. (They were, however, egregiously wrong to suggest that this would not have been true if an ordinary citizen had been treated in the same way.)

3   The elements of punishment

In Part I of this book I defended a denunciatory account of punishment; and in arguing that 'perp walks' are a form of punishment I am interested in showing that they turn out to be a form of punishment on precisely this account. However, the strategy I adopt will be one that also shows that even if one does not accept the denunciatory account one should still regard perp walks as a form of punishment. In fact, it will turn out that the denunciatory account of punishment makes it harder, rather than easier, to argue that perp walks are a form of punishment (although they will ultimately turn out to be one). This is worth noticing for the

---

[2] Davies 2011; Willsher and Rushe 2011.
[3] Levy 2011.

following straightforward reason. My view that punishment constitutively involves a denunciatory expressive component is controversial. If my argument that perp walks are a form of punishment depended on it in a significant manner, then this would weakens my chances of showing those who do not accept this view that perp walks are a form of punishment. Since I take this to be a significant normative conclusion, with non-trivial practical implications, it is worth arguing for it in a way that makes it depend on as few controversial premises as possible. For this reason, I shall consider two kinds of view of punishment in this chapter: those which involve what I shall call a 'Minimal Conception' of Punishment, and members of what I shall call the 'Expressive Family' of views. A wide range of views, including the one that I defended in Part I, can be located within this conceptual space.

On the Minimal Conception of Punishment (henceforth MC) punishment is harsh treatment, inflicted on a wrongdoer or suspected wrongdoer, by an appropriate authority, in response to specifiable wrongdoing.[4] MC consists of four conditions which are individually necessary and jointly sufficient for a form of treatment to constitute punishment. I shall refer to these conditions as the MCPs. I refer to MC as a 'conception' of punishment rather than a definition or account, because its content is somewhat indeterminate. In particular, the notion of harshness could be spelled out in a number of ways. For example, we might take treatment's being 'harsh' to require that it actually harm an offender; or that it harm them in some specific way – for example, in ways that involve depriving them of liberty or in ways that infringe rights which they either have, or would have in circumstances in which they had committed no crime.

David Boonin has recently put forward an account of punishment which seems closely related to MC. Boonin characterizes punishment as 'intentionally inflicted authorized retributive reprobative harm'.[5] Boonin also requires that punishment involves 'intentionally inflicted harm'. This seems to be a way of making the idea that punishment must involve harsh treatment more determinate. (We shall also see in a moment that it does so in a somewhat problematic manner.) Boonin's requirement that punishment be 'authorized' corresponds to the third MCP. Furthermore, his discussion of the idea that punishment must be 'retributive' suggests that he takes this to require only that the

---

[4] Hart 1959.
[5] Boonin 2008 p. 23.

punishment is a response to some specific wrongdoing: the second and fourth of the MCPs. What Boonin adds to the MCPs is the requirement that punishment be 'reprobative': in other words that it should express official condemnation of wrongdoing. This aligns him with the Expressive Family of Views, which I shall now discuss.

From the point of view of this book MC overlooks a significant feature of punishment: its expressive dimension. In Chapter 2 I argued that in order to avoid the abolitionist arguments put forward by Hanna and Boonin, we should incorporate an expressive element into the definition of punishment; and in Chapters 3 and 4 I argued that the kinds of expressive consideration that were required involved denunciation to a wider political community, rather than communication to an offender. But for the time being it will be convenient to take account of both communicative and denunciatory views, and regard them as being members of a larger family of expressive views which I call EF.

According to members of EF, a way of treating offenders only constitutes punishment if it satisfies both the MCPs and some further expressive condition or conditions, which I shall refer to as Putative Expressive Conditions, or PECs. So EF includes both denunciatory views like my own, where the primary target of the communication is the society whose laws an offender has offended against, and communicative views, like Duff's on which the principal target of penal communication is the offender.[6] EF can also include two kinds of hybrid view. On Conjunctive Hybrid views, harsh treatment constitutes punishment only if it satisfies the MCPs and is intended to convey a message both to an offender and to a wider society. On Disjunctive Hybrid Views, a form of harsh treatment constitutes punishment provided it satisfies the MCPs and is intended to communicate something to *either* the offender or a wider society of which the offender is a part. However for the purposes of this chapter, I shall exclude what I called 'audience-independent expressivism' from EF since I take the arguments of Chapter 4 to have shown it to be untenable.

4 Minimal conditions for punishment (1): harsh treatment

Many philosophers hold that something can only constitute a case of punishment if it involves harsh treatment of someone who is taken

---

[6] Duff 2001; Metz 2000.

to have committed an offense.[7] On an everyday understanding of the notion of harshness, perp walks will typically involve harsh treatment. They are liable to be experienced as humiliating and shameful, and in many cases – perhaps including the one involving Strauss-Kahn which I described at the beginning of this paper – it seems plausible that they are intended in precisely this way.

Some philosophers hold that punishment must involve an intention to cause suffering to the individual on whom it is inflicted.[8] We might regard this as a way to further specify the notion of harshness involved in the MCPs.[9] However, I have already argued in Chapter 2 that this conception of harshness is unsatisfactory, at least in the context of the current debate. So we should not understand the notion of harshness in this way.

One might hold that punishment must involve some sort of abridgement of someone's rights; or a restriction on someone's liberty.[10] I shall treat these as ways of specifying the notion of 'harshness' involved in the MCPs more precisely. Whatever the merits of such accounts of punishment, they do not seem to present any special obstacle to the view that perp walks constitute a form of punishment. First notice that, on pain of implausibility, the notions of 'restriction of liberty' and 'infringement of rights' must be understood in a way that avoids entailing that post-trial imprisonment is not a form of punishment. It is hard to interpret these ideas in a way that means that post-trial imprisonment is not a form of punishment but that perp walks are.

---

[7] One anonymous reader suggested that the 'harsh treatment' condition should be understood as requiring that punishment involve harsh treatment inflicted on someone who has been convicted of an offense. On this view perp walks of the sort I am concerned with would not constitute punishment. I find this view unhelpful, since it obscures rather than clarifies the role which conviction plays in the legal system. We typically take conviction to play a role in making it legitimate to treat someone in a way in which it would not otherwise be legitimate to treat them. This point is naturally expressed by saying that conviction legitimates punishment. On the referee's suggested way of seeing things we cannot say this. We might say instead that conviction legitimates punishment* where punishment* is anything that satisfies all the conditions for being punishment other than the condition of being imposed on a convicted offender. Those who are attracted to the referee's way of seeing things are invited to substitute 'punishment*' for 'punishment' until the final section of this chapter. The practical upshot – that this form of treatment is illegitimate – will be the same.

[8] Hanna 2008; Boonin 2008.

[9] Cf. Hanna 2008.

[10] I thank an anonymous reader for this suggestion.

Thus one might argue that perp walks involve an infringement of relatively uncontroversial rights, such as a right of freedom of movement or of freedom of association. However, many people hold that an individual's rights in these areas are not necessarily taken to have been abridged when their exercise is made subject to the constraints of duly-made law. (Thus the existence of speed limits in built-up areas is not reasonably understood as involving an infringement of my right to freedom of movement.) Someone might hold that the sorts of restrictions on movement and association that perp walks involve can be appropriately understood in an analogous way. However on a view of this sort it is not clear that post-trial imprisonment constitutes an infringement of rights, since the restrictions that those who are imprisoned undergo are imposed by duly imposed law.

Similarly, perp walks seem to involve restrictions on an individual's liberty, since they involve fairly obvious constraints on an individual's capacities for unconstrained movement. Someone might propose a conception of liberty under which such constraints did not necessarily amount to a restriction of liberty properly understood. Consider, for example, Hobbes' view of liberty, on which physical constraints on movement only restrict my liberty when I am trying to escape. However it is not clear that someone could propose a view of this sort on which post-trial imprisonment did count as a restriction of liberty. (As, on Hobbes view, it does not.)

5 Minimal conditions of punishment (2): response to specifiable wrongdoing

Even if perp walks do involve harsh treatment, we might nevertheless wonder whether they involve a response to 'specifiable wrongdoing'. There are two questions to consider: 'Can perp walks be seen as a response to wrongdoing, rather than something less, such as the suspicion of wrongdoing?' and 'Can they be regarded as responses to *specifiable* wrongdoing?' [11]

---

[11] Someone might argue that even if perp walks are not responses to specifiable wrongdoing, it is sufficient for a critic of the practice to establish that they are a response to a suspicion of wrongdoing, and then to argue that they are a form of treatment which is analogous to punishment but which is inflicted when a much lower evidential burden is met. I think that a full exploration of this line of argument would require a consideration of the role that the existence of a strong evidential burden plays in justifying the harsh treatment punishment involves. Space precludes me from discussing these complex issues in detail.

Perp walks can be inflicted on individuals who are, in fact, innocent of any offense. Someone might conclude from this that they cannot be a response to wrongdoing. This argument presupposes that something cannot be a response to wrongdoing if it can occur without any actual wrongdoing taking place. However, this conception of a response to wrongdoing differs from the one intended by someone who holds that punishment must be a response to wrongdoing. Consider the case of an innocent person who is found guilty and has penal sanctions inflicted upon them. We should not deny that in such a case an innocent person was being punished. If we did, we would be unable to say that they were being *wrongly* punished.[12]

The notion of a response to wrongdoing that is required in this context is normatively freighted. On this conception it follows from A's being a response to B that the occurrence of B is regarded as a reason for A. This does not entail that A cannot occur without B having occurred. It entails that if B occurs without A having occurred, a mistake has been made.

The penal sanctions we impose on those found guilty by the courts are correctly understood as responses to wrongdoing in this sense. In a civilized society, the fact that someone is shown to have been innocent of a crime that they are alleged to have committed is regarded as a reason for making some kind of public acknowledgment of their innocence and the wrongfulness of having inflicted harsh treatment on them.

Some societies find it difficult to make the kind of public acknowledgment which a conception of punishment as a response to wrongdoing seems to call for in such cases.[13] We might extrapolate from this to the possibility of a society which never acknowledges mistakes of this sort: for example, a society with legal institutions which do not allow even for the possibility of appealing against a sentence. If my view entailed

---

[12] Someone might argue that the relationship between 'wrongful punishment' and punishment proper should be seen as analogous to that between a rubber duck and a real duck. Rubber ducks provide no counter-example to the claim that ducks are living creatures – they are things which merely purport to be ducks. Some instances of wrongful punishment might be understood that way – for example, ones in which harsh treatment is inflicted in full knowledge of the innocence of the supposed perpetrator. But not all instances of the punishment of the innocent are like this.

[13] Consider Lord Denning's notorious remark, concerning the later-exonerated 'Birmingham Six', that to accept that the police had given false testimony against them would open an 'appalling vista'. (In fairness, it should be noted that Denning later recanted this view.) (Cf. Dyer 1999.)

that a society of this sort could not be regarded as punishing people, it would be unacceptably counterintuitive.

Fortunately, it does not. We should distinguish possible cases here. One is a society which acknowledges the potential fallibility of its legal institutions and pays lip-service to the idea that, ideally speaking, the innocent should not be punished. It appeals to the imperfection of all practicable human institutions to justify the view that on the whole, it is better if those who are found guilty are not exonerated. Here it seems appropriate to think of sanctions being imposed as a response to wrong-doing, and hence that the society has institutions of punishment – albeit ones which have gone badly awry. More fantastically, perhaps, we can imagine a society which does not countenance the possibility of judges making mistakes. Here too, we might legitimately regard sanctions as being imposed in response to wrongdoing, and so as constituting something which we can recognize as punishment, although the case is sufficiently alien that in doing so, one might be moved to comment on some of the ways in which the institutions of this society differ from our own.

Here is a more difficult case. Judges are known and acknowledged to be fallible. However there is no institutional basis for recognizing cases where mistakes have been made, and no acknowledgment that mistakes of this sort present even a *prima facie* reason for suspending sanctions, acknowledging that they have been wrongly imposed, or compensating those on whom they are imposed. We might deny that in this case sanctions are being imposed as a response to wrongdoing: it seems as though they are, rather, imposed as a response to justified suspicion of wrong-doing. What makes the difference is that in a case like this, there seems no reason for anyone to think that those who have imposed the sanction take themselves to have acted inappropriately in the absence of actual wrongdoing.

These hypothetical cases are intended to shed light on the question of whether perp walks can be regarded as a response to wrongdoing or merely as a response to suspected wrongdoing. If they are analogous to the first kind of case then the answer is 'Yes'. If they are analogous to the third kind of case the answer appears to be 'No'. (It seems fairly clear that they are not analogous to the second kind of case.) One might suppose that they are analogous to the third kind of case, insofar as there seems to be little institutional scope for public acknowledgment of cases of wrongful arrest.

However, matters are not quite so simple. It is not plausible to suppose that there is nothing normatively inappropriate about individuals who turn out to be innocent being subjected to perp walks. Admittedly, the idea that law enforcement officials should admit that they have made a mistake in such cases might not seem to enjoy much popular support. However, we should not make too much of this. One thing we might want to consider is that a formal finding that an individual is not guilty is itself a public acknowledgment of the sort we are looking for.

Of course, not all those who are arrested on grounds of reasonable suspicion without being found guilty end up being acquitted in a court of law: sometimes charges are dropped and a case does not come to trial. Does our practice in such cases undermine the case for seeing perp walks as a response to wrongdoing rather than to the mere suspicion of wrongdoing? It need not. An alternative understanding of our practice would be one on which we take it that the *prima facie* case for acknowledging that a sanction has been wrongly imposed is outweighed by public policy considerations, such as the importance of not undermining either the morale of law enforcement officers or the trust that the public places in them.[14] This way of seeing things would make cases of this sort analogous to the first kind of fictitious case I discussed above.

I have argued that perp walks should be seen as involving a response to wrongdoing rather than as a response to the reasonable suspicion of wrongdoing. One might, nevertheless wonder whether they can be seen as a response to *specifiable* wrongdoing. One *prima facie* point in favor of the idea that they can is that in many countries individuals enjoy various kinds of constitutional and legal protections against arbitrary arrest. Such provisions normally require that arrests should only take place on the basis of some reasonable cause. Requirements that individuals should be charged with a specific offense within a given time frame add to the case for thinking that insofar as we have something which is a response to wrongdoing, it is a response to specifiable wrongdoing.

However individuals are not always tried for offenses they are initially charged with. Practices such as plea-bargaining can only make sense in a system where this is both true and publicly acknowledged. This fact might appear to undermine the idea that perp walks involve a response to *specifiable* wrongdoing. It might seem as though they are better understood as involving a response to wrongdoing somewhere in the vicinity of the offense with which the individual is charged. This point is less significant than it might appear at first sight. The fact that an individual need not be prosecuted for an offense that they are initially

---

[14] This is not to concede that such considerations should be decisive, but simply to acknowledge the possibility that in many cases they are.

charged with need not indicate that the perp walk is not intended as a response to that kind of wrongdoing. It shows only that, if convicted, their sentence is not a response to the same wrongdoing that their initial treatment was. This is not especially paradoxical. There would only be a paradox if we wanted to maintain that the perp walk and the eventual punishment should be seen as responses to the same punishment. Someone defending my view should not claim this: apart from anything else it would be difficult to see what we should say about individuals who ended up not being charged at all, and about individuals who were subsequently found innocent.

6 Minimal conditions of punishment (3): appropriate authority

Let us now consider the 'appropriate authority' component of the MCPs. It is tempting to say that an appropriate authority is simply an authority which has the right to inflict punishment. We could then argue that perp walks are not punishment simply on the grounds that they involve treatment which is typically inflicted by agents of law enforcement such as the police, and that it is not properly part of the police's role to inflict punishment. However, if the appropriate authority condition is intended as part of a definition of punishment, we cannot understand it in the way suggested, on pain of circularity.[15]

Someone might claim the police are accorded authority to investigate crimes and to arrest suspects but not to subject them to humiliating treatment. They might then deny that humiliating treatment of the sort we are considering here is punishment, since the police are not authorized to treat people in this way. Someone who held this view would owe us a non-circular account of the appropriate authority condition. This account would be one on which the question of whether the appropriate authority condition was satisfied would depend not only on the status of the person inflicting the treatment, but also on whether they had the authority to inflict treatment of precisely that sort.

We should not accept an account of this sort. Consider a case in which the death penalty (or some other way of treating the convicted) is ruled

---

[15] This point does not preclude us from turning the argument round. If we establish that perp walks *are* punishment, this would be a reason for denying that law enforcement officers should subject suspects to them, provided we had independent grounds for saying that law enforcement officers should not be in the job of meting out punishment.

unconstitutional under an existing constitution. If it is unconstitutional, no judge had the authority to impose it. It contributes neither to clarity nor to justice to claim that those on whom it was inflicted were not punished. But this is what the suggestion commits us to.

Here is a non-circular explication of the notion of an appropriate authority. An authority is 'appropriate' in this context when and only when it has been accorded the right to inflict harsh treatment of the sort in question. To say that an individual or group is accorded a right is to say that they are regarded as or acknowledged as having the right by some group who acknowledge the set of rules which specify the offense for which the individual is being punished.[16,17]

If the 'appropriate authority' condition is understood in this way, perp walks will often satisfy it. They are public events that are taken to be legitimate by law enforcement officials, by journalists and photographers, and by the public at large. They are not challenged in the courts, and they only rarely attract critical public commentary. Furthermore, since there is no attempt to hide what is going on, we cannot classify them as events that are merely tacitly condoned while being formally frowned on. In short, everything suggests that we do accord to law enforcement officials the right to inflict this treatment on those suspected of wrongdoing.

7   The expressive conditions

I have now argued that perp walks could be seen as satisfying the MCPs. Since it is normally inappropriate for officials of a state, acting in their capacity as representatives of the state, to inflict punishment prior to a criminal trial, those who think that the MCPs provide us with an

---

[16] It does not follow from the fact that an individual or group of individuals is accorded or acknowledged as having a right by a group that they actually do have such a right. So understanding the 'appropriate authority' condition in the way that I suggest does not foreclose the possibility that either individual instances of punishment or our punitive institutions as a whole might turn out to be illegitimate.

[17] It follows that 'appropriate' authorities may include all kinds of bodies that we might not normally regard as having the right to inflict *legal* punishment – teachers, parents, sports referees, gang bosses, and so on. I take this to be a positive feature of my account: it seems plausible that penalties inflicted for rules infractions by such individuals are rightly referred to as punishments, even if they cannot be justified in the same ways that we take legal punishment to be justified. (Cf. Duff 2001: for a contrasting view, see Brooks 2012.)

adequate characterization of punishment ought to find the institution problematic.

However, I have argued in Chapter 2 at MCPs give us an inadequate characterization of punishment. There are practices which satisfy the MCPs, such as the arrest and pre-trial confinement by the state of those suspected of wrongdoing, which seem to be unavoidable from a practical point of view – and to that extent morally justifiable – if the law is to be enforced at all; and yet these are conceptually distinct from punishment. On the account of harshness I have given, pre-trial confinement of suspects is harsh; it is also inflicted by an appropriate authority; it is, also plausibly characterized as a response to wrongdoing, in the normative sense of response which I outlined in Section 4.

As we saw in Chapter 2, considerations of this sort should lead us to prefer a version of EF to MCP. However, we might wonder whether incorporating one or more PECs into our conception of punishment might give us grounds for denying that perp walks are a form of punishment. In the remainder of this chapter, I shall argue that they do not.

8   Perp walks and the denunciatory account

I have used the label 'denunciatory' to refer to accounts of punishment on which: (1) the expressive goals of a form of harsh treatment are essential to classifying it as punishment; and (2) it is sufficient for the treatment's counting as punishment that it should include among the intended recipients of the message communicated members of a political community subject to the law in response to a violation of which the harsh treatment is imposed other than the person being punished.

This characterization of denunciatory accounts of punishment says very little about the content that has to be expressed by the harsh treatment. In Chapter 3, I argued that the most plausible denunciatory accounts were ones which aimed to communicate that a particular offender had engaged in a particular form of wrongdoing. At this point it may be worth adding two further points. The first is that even a denunciatory conception punishment need not aim at shaming the offender. Secondly, we need not assume that on a denunciatory account, punishment can have no other goals than that of expressing a message of a particular sort – or even that it can have no other communicative goals.[18]

---

[18] Thus, what Thom Brooks has called a 'unified' theory of punishment, on which punishment is justified insofar as it achieves one of a number of different goals, might still count as a denunciatory account in my terms.

On a denunciatory account of punishment, perp walks seem to constitute a form of punishment. The purpose of the perp walk seems to be, precisely, to display the individual who is subjected to it as being someone who has behaved in such a way as to merit investigation and custody. Furthermore, at least in cases like Strauss-Kahn's, the intended audience seems to include – though it need not be limited to – members of a political community who are subject to the law that the individual in question is accused of breaking.

One might resist this conclusion in one of two ways. First one might argue that although the perp walk does have an expressive purpose, the expressive purpose which it involves is distinct from that which is characteristic of punishment. It is the entirely legitimate purpose of communicating to the public the fact that one particular individual is being investigated.

However, this seems incorrect. I argued earlier in this chapter that perp walks involve harsh treatment. There are many ways in which the relevant information could be communicated that would not count as harsh treatment. (e.g., the names of offenders and their offenses might be entered in a database on a publicly available webpage.) There might be classes of offenders whose typical members were unfazed by this. On my account of harshness, they would not be harshly treated.) Furthermore, the institution of the perp walk is one in which it is made conspicuous that putative offenders are being treated in ways whose normal justification depends on their having engaged in wrongdoing.

In the light of this, two things seem to follow. The first is that it would be unreasonable for those who take the display of harshness involved in the perp walk to be aimed at them to take it as being nothing more than a way of communicating to them that certain individuals were under investigation. The second is that it would be reasonable for them to take it that the individuals had engaged in some forms of wrongdoing that normally justify treatment of this sort. But to say this is to say, at least on the sorts of Gricean account of communication that we considered in Chapter 3, that they communicate a kind of message which is characteristic of punishment.

Someone might resist the conclusion that on a denunciatory account perp walks should count as a form of punishment on different grounds. They could argue that although perp walks do involve putting a putative offender on display before a certain kind of audience, they do so in a way that makes the role of that audience, and communication with that audience, incidental and inessential. The idea here would be that the perp walk was aimed at making the offender feel ashamed. On this account it would be true that perp walks had an expressive purpose, but it would be an expressive purpose on which the intended recipient of the message was not a wider political community but the putative offender him- or herself. On this view perp walks would not necessarily meet the conditions for constituting a form of punishment, as conceived by denunciatory accounts.

However, this response is unsatisfactory. Suppose the purpose of perp walks is to shame putative offenders. The mechanism envisaged for bringing this about is one whereby the individual comes to feel shame because they recognize that a certain audience regards them in a particular way. If the recognition of this fact is part of the mechanism that is intended here, then perp walks have an expressive goal which involves communicating something to an audience. If they did not do so, then the envisaged mechanism could not work: there would be nothing of the right sort for the offender to recognize. So a denunciatory account of punishment can cover cases of this sort.

Here is an objection. There are ways of inducing shame in a putative offender which would not involve their recognition that a particular audience sees them in a particular way. (Thus, for example, one might try to get a putative offender to imagine that a certain audience sees them in a particular way.) So even if perp walks are aimed at shaming putative offenders, doing so need not involve communicating a message to a wider audience. It may be enough that the putative offender believe (or even imagine) that they are so seen. Since perp walks could achieve the goal of getting putative offenders to feel shame without succeeding in communicating a message about the shamefulness of the putative offender to that audience, someone who aims to shame an offender by making them engage in a perp walk need not intend to communicate a message to an audience.

We can certainly imagine cases in which putative offenders end up feeling shame, even though they are mistaken about how they are seen by an external audience. However this is not enough to show that the institution of the perp walk doesn't involve an intention to communicate with such an audience. It is a case of someone achieving a goal by an unintended means. The objection requires us to imagine a situation in which perp walks were intended to produce shame in putative offenders without an intention to communicate anything to an audience.

Consider another kind of case: a society in which it is widely known among those who engage in law enforcement that members of the public are more or less indifferent to displays of putative offenders, but where this is not typically known to those arrested, so that the perp walk is a reliable means of inducing shame in offenders. Here the perp walk could be intended to induce shame in perpetrators without there being an intention to convey anything to an audience.

It is hard to see how this kind of situation could be stable: to imagine it, we need to imagine a society in which there is no overlap and little social commerce between arrestees and law enforcement officials. The society being imagined also would be one in which there was an extreme lack of transparency in its social institutions. If we concede that in such a society perp walks would not be a form of punishment, then we are not making the same concession about actual societies, or indeed about any society we should want to live in.

We might believe that if we think that perp walks are a form of punishment in our society, then we should be prepared to count closely analogous forms of treatment in imaginably different forms of society as forms of punishment as well. This approach begs the question against denunciatory forms of punishment. It is tantamount to insisting that questions about how a certain form of treatment is understood by society at large are irrelevant to whether or not we should classify something as punishment.

9　Communicative accounts

I have now argued that on both a minimal conception of punishment as well as the denunciatory account I have been defending in this book, we should see perp walks as constituting a form of punishment. Although it is not central to the argument of this book, I now want to argue that all advocates of communicative versions of expressivism should also accept a similar conclusion. On a communicative account, the intended recipient is the individual on whom harsh treatment is inflicted.

As we have seen, the most prominent contemporary advocate of a communicative view is Antony Duff.[19] He holds that it is partially constitutive of a form of harsh treatment's constituting punishment that it should have an expressive dimension. He also holds that the harsh treatment which punishment involves should be aimed at bringing about remorse and or regret on the part of the offender. One might think that on this view there would be a fairly straightforward strategy for arguing against the claim that perp walks are a form of punishment. For one might argue that perp walks do not, or need not, have such an aim. The case for thinking this might be bolstered by some of the considerations put forward in the previous section in favor of the claim that the intended audience in such a case is not the perpetrator but the community at large.

---

[19] Duff 2001, 2009.

This would be a good argument if we construed Duff's view as being one on which it is not only constitutive of something's being punishment that it should have an expressive dimension, but also constitutive of its being punishment that it be intended to express a message of a particular sort to a particular recipient. However, this seems implausible.[20]

Here is a more plausible alternative. Suppose we distinguish carefully between the project of explaining what punishment is and the project of explaining why it is sometimes justified. Then there are two distinguishable claims we might make about the expressive dimension of punishment, one broader and one more narrow. The broader claim is that punishment must have an expressive dimension; the narrower one that it must be intended to express a message of a certain sort to a certain audience.

Duff seems to be committed to regarding the broader expressive claim as being one which articulates something which is partly constitutive of punishment.[21] However, it seems possible to do so without regarding the second claim as also being partly constitutive of punishment. One might instead regard it as something which needs to be the case in order for certain forms of punishment to be justified.

This view seems at least as well supported as an account on which narrow expressive claims are built into the definition of punishment. The sorts of arguments which expressivists typically rely on to support the claim that punishment must have an expressive dimension, such as Feinberg's appeal to the distinction between punishments and taxes, seem unable to support the suggestion that particular communicative goals must be constitutive of punishment.[22] Furthermore a view on which the narrower claims about punishment are seen as partially constitutive of something's being punishment seem to run in to difficulty when we consider cases such as capital punishment. On a reading of Duff's view where the narrow expressive conditions are constitutive of punishment, many cases of capital punishment might fail to constitute punishment at all. This seems implausible. By contrast, on the account which I am proposing we can hold that capital punishment is indeed

---

[20] One reason why it seems implausible is that the sorts of communicative intentions that Duff has in mind seem to be closely bound up with notions of repentance and forgiveness, which seem to be far from being culturally universal. Thus, for example, Konstan 2012 argues that the notion of forgiveness cannot be found among the ancient Greeks, in early Judaism or even in the Church fathers. It seems implausible to claim that punishment was unknown in such societies.

[21] Duff 2009.

[22] Feinberg 1970.

punishment, but it is a form of punishment which will almost always be unjustified.[23]

On this way of understanding Duff's view, perp walks can also count as a form of punishment. And if Duff is right about the conditions which must be satisfied for a form of punishment to be justified, they will, in many cases, be problematic from a normative point of view for two distinct reasons. They will be unjustified both because they are inflicted in advance of a criminal trial and because they aim at sending a message to the wrong recipient.

10 Hybrid views

In Section 3 I introduced and defined two kinds of 'hybrid' members of EF: disjunctive and conjunctive hybrids. On a disjunctive hybrid view it will be sufficient for a form of harsh treatment which satisfies the MCPs to constitute punishment that it be directed at an audience consisting of members of the political community to whom the offender belongs. In other words, a disjunctive hybrid view is just a particular version of a denunciatory view as that is defined in Section 7. So the arguments I have used to show that denunciatory accounts entail that perp walks are a form of punishment apply without modification.

Conjunctive hybrid views raise more difficult concerns. Since they are not versions of the denunciatory view, the arguments of Section 6 do not show that on such views perp walks must be a form of punishment. However, there is more to say. In Section 7, I argued against views on which it is a necessary condition for a form of harsh treatment's constituting punishment that it should be aimed at expressing a message to an offender. I suggested that views of this sort were a less satisfactory way of developing the underlying insights of the communicative view than views on which the fact that the message expressed was to an offender played a role in justifying the institution of punishment, but was not constitutive of that institution. Conjunctive hybrid views are views on which this is a necessary condition of a form of harsh treatment's constituting punishment. So the points made in Section 7 apply to them as well. The possibility of such views makes relatively little difference to my analysis as a whole.

---

[23] A further reason for taking the communicative view in the way I have suggested is that it makes it easier to see how certain non-paradigmatic cases of punishment, such as the punishment of war criminals and business corporations might constitute punishment. See Chapters 7 and 8 for further discussion.

11 Concluding remarks

I have argued that on both a minimal conception of punishment and on the most plausible members of the expressive family, we should regard perp walks as constituting a form of punishment. We might wonder what the practical upshot of this conclusion is. Does it follow that there is something morally objectionable about the practice?

It does. One quick route to this conclusion would be to argue that it is wrong to punish someone without a fair criminal trial. But there is a natural follow-up to this question. We might ask what it is about criminal trials that makes them, rather than any other form of investigative procedure, the necessary preliminary to legitimate punishment. This question might seem especially pressing when we bear in mind that individuals do not become the subject of criminal indictments on the basis of mere suspicion. One might think that there is good reason to think that many indicted criminals are guilty of something even before a formal finding of guilt has been made.

Any adequate answer to this question would require something that goes well beyond the current book, namely a theory of the criminal trial. Such a theory would contain at least two parts. First, it would explain what distinguishes criminal trials from other forms of proceeding. One plausible form of answer would make reference to the requirement for a particularly high standard of proof. Secondly, it would explain why there is a normative link between this distinctive form of trial and liability to punishment. I leave it as an open question how an advocate of a denunciatory account of punishment might answer this question.

We might also ask whether the account I have put forward has any other practical implications. It is at least plausible that some other common forms of law enforcement practices – such as the widespread distribution of suspects' mugshots and their detention in prison-like conditions – might be subject to the same form of criticism.[24] The same might also be true of some aspects of the trial process – for example, the setting of the court room, the entering of formal pleas, and the fact the plea made is that of 'not guilty' rather than 'innocent'.[25,26]

---

[24] I am indebted to an anonymous referee for this journal for this suggestion.

[25] I am indebted to a (different) anonymous referee for these suggestions and to Duff 1986 for the general suggestion that the trial has an expressive dimension.

[26] Bass 2002, Luban 2007 and Wringe 2006 all suggest that war crimes trials have an important expressive dimension, which is relevant to their justifiability. The same may also be true of trials of other high-profile public figures. If this is correct, then it is also important to ensure that the expressive dimensions of such trials do not transform them into instances of punishment without trial.

It is worth entering two caveats here. One is that the extent to which an expressive theory of punishment requires us to regard these features of the criminal justice process as forms of punishment is likely to depend to some extent on the details of the expressive theory. Thus, for example it will be hard to defend the view that aspects of the treatment of those who are being detained for trial that are not widely known should be regarded as having a denunciatory function (though they might have a communicative function).

A second *caveat* anticipates a further objection. Someone might worry that if we pursue the analysis proposed in this paper to the fullest extent possible, it will turn out that so many aspects of our system of criminal justice turn out to be forms of punishment that avoiding pre-trial punishment might involve giving up on the pursuit of criminal justice altogether.

This would be so, for example, if arresting a suspect constituted a form of punishment – a consequence that might be thought to constitute a *reductio* of the view proposed here.

This line of argument seems more likely to succeed when directed at versions of MCP than expressive views. I noted in Section 7 that one advantage of expressive views is that they leave room to argue that pre-trial detention of suspected offenders need not count as punishment. Something similar seems to be true of arresting a subject: there seems no need to assume that it must have either a communicatory or a denunciatory function (although it may be carried out in a way which ensures that it does). It may nevertheless turn out that in practice certain aspects of our system of criminal law enforcement do impose punishments where they should not do so. If so, they need and deserve reform.[27] But to concede this is not to concede the full force of the objection. [28]

---

[27] It is also worth observing that the criminal trial in particular can be regarded as having features such as the presumption of innocence whose expressive dimension seem to go some way towards distinguishing it from anything that might be regarded as a form of punishment.

[28] I would like to thank Sandrine Berges, Nathan Hanna, Saladin Meckled-Garcia, Ambrose Lee, an audience at the 2013 meeting of the Association for Social and Legal Philosophy and two anonymous referees for the journal *Ethical Theory and Moral Practice* for comments on earlier drafts of this chapter.

6
Punishing War Crimes

1 Introduction

In the first half of this book, I defended a denunciatory version of an expressive theory of punishment, as applied to paradigmatic case of punishment: that in which a state is punishing one of its own citizens. The plausibility of the account of punishment I developed there depended, at least to some extent, on the idea that – in the paradigmatic case – an offender who is punished is a member of the political community which expresses its commitment to a set of norms by inflicting harsh treatment on him or her.

However, there are many cases of punishment which do not resemble the paradigmatic case in every respect. Some of these are cases which we do not typically recognize as involving punishment, such as the case of perp walks, which we considered in Chapter 5. But others are cases which we would naturally recognize as instances of punishment – and indeed of justifiable punishment. Such cases are both philosophically interesting and practically challenging. We might reasonably hope that an adequate theoretical account of punishment might shed some light on the questions which they raise.

In this chapter I consider one kind of case of this sort: the punishment of war crimes (and other breaches of international criminal law) by international tribunals. The kinds of case I have in mind here are best exemplified by the cases adjudicated by the International Criminal Tribunal for the Former Yugoslavia and the International Criminal Tribunal for Rwanda. Such trials, and the punishments imposed on at least some offenders at their end, are widely viewed as being, in some sense legitimate. However, giving an explanation of how they can be is a much trickier issue: and as we shall see, there is at least some reason for thinking that any such attempts must fail.

The views that I put forward in this chapter will draw on the denunciatory version of expressivism that I defended in the first half of this book. However, it will not be a straightforward 'application' of the denunciatory view to the case of war crimes. We should not ignore the extent to which the punishment of such crimes departs from the paradigmatic case of punishment, nor the extent to which this fact reflects on the normative status of such punishments. The account that I offer will differ from the account I have given of the paradigmatic case of punishment in significant respects. In particular it will lay stress on the expressive significance of the trial in a way that my account of the paradigmatic case of punishment did not.

My interest here is in defending practices of holding war criminals to account which already exist. Some might suggest the considerations about Victor's Justice that I shall be discussing show that the punishment of war criminals could only be justified if we were to develop international tribunals, which would then allow for the impartial punishment of participants on both sides of any conflict. However, this seems a somewhat utopian prospect. It is not simply that such tribunals do not currently exist. There seem to be strong practical barriers to their implementation: it seems highly unlikely that powerful nations would be willing to hand over their citizens to such tribunals except in circumstances where military defeat or diplomatic failure left them with no other option. That being so, it seems worth investigating the question of whether the institutions we have succeeded in putting into place might be able to escape the Victor's Justice objection.[1]

2   Expressivism and the punishment of war crimes

As we have seen, expressive theories have come in both communicative and denunciatory varieties. On communicative views, the intended audience for the communication is, at least in the first instance, the wrongdoer. On my denunciatory view the intended audience may be considerably wider – not just, or even primarily the wrongdoer, but the society itself – or even the world at large.

---

[1] The arguments of this chapter supersede those of Wringe 2006 which I now find unsatisfactory for reasons outlined in sections 4 below. For an earlier rethinking of my position, also somewhat unsatisfactory, see Wringe 2010, parts of which are incorporated into this chapter.

Expressive theories of the sort that I have been discussing in this book may seem untenable here. My defense of the denunciatory view detailed in Chapter 3 relied heavily on the idea that punishment involves the state's expressing a message to citizens. However war criminals are often – perhaps even typically – tried and sentenced by citizens of states other than their own. For this reason, it is at least initially unclear how the account I developed there can be applied to the punishment of war criminals by international tribunals or even the International Criminal Court (ICC).

This problem also arises for communicative versions of expressivism, such as Antony Duff's. On Duff's view, the legitimacy of punishment depends on the person receiving the punishment being a member of the community against whose norms he has offended. The paradigmatic example of such a community, and the one that Duff seems most often to have in mind, is of course the contemporary liberal state.[2] Nothing Duff says rules out the possibility of other communities – and in particular international community's – existing. Nevertheless this feature of his account makes it difficult to see how it could be extended to provide a justification of the punishment of war criminals.

I noted earlier that the punishment of war crimes might involve citizens of one state being punished by citizens of another state. However, it does not follow from this that there might not be some wider community that war criminals and those who punish them might both be members of. Two individuals who are members of distinct communities of one sort might share membership of a wider community. For example two individuals might be members of different academic institutions while being citizens of the same state. Similarly, we might think that individuals who are citizens of distinct states are nevertheless members of some further community which extends beyond the borders of their state.

We often take states to be the most extensive communities to which individuals belong. However, we need not do so. Citizens of two distinct European states which are both members of the European Union might see themselves as belonging to a European community which extends beyond national boundaries. To the extent that they are subject to a common set of regulations and shared institutions, and share a common political culture, they are correct to do so.

---

[2] Duff does consider other kinds of community such as monasteries and universities. However, the point of doing so seems to be as a way of providing support for his conclusions about punishment within a liberal state.

It does not follow from this point that war criminals will always belong to the same community as those who seek to punish them. To ensure this, we need some notion of a world community, to which all human beings belong. Antony Duff has suggested it is enough for an advocate of communicative theories of punishment if both the punisher and the person being punished are members of a single moral community. He expands on this suggestion by alluding first to the Kantian notion of a 'Kingdom of Ends' and secondly – in language which suggests that he finds the notion more appealing – to Rai Gaita's suggestion that human beings should be seen as members of a single community in virtue of their 'common humanity'.[3]

This seems insufficient. If the arguments that I put forward in Chapter 3 were correct, then it seems as though talk of punishment will only be appropriate when it is appropriate to think of the individual enforcing the standards as speaking on behalf of the community in question.[4] Who is authorized to speak on behalf of the moral community of mankind? The most obvious answers are 'anybody' and 'nobody'. Neither seems satisfactory: if nobody is authorized to speak, then we seem to lose any grip on the idea that we can talk of punishment in this context; if anyone is authorized to speak, then we seem to leave open the door to vigilante justice.

Two other answers also seem problematic: that the righteous, or morally good, are authorized to speak on behalf of the human community; and that the victims of wrongdoing are. The first puts many of those who, in practice institute war crimes trials, into a position that is apt to make them seem unsustainably hubristic; and the second seems to leave open the possibility of too many kinds of violation being effectively unpunishable.

---

[3] I take the notion of 'common humanity' as one that goes beyond ascribing human beings membership in a single community in virtue of a common property in the austere metaphysical sense of property: part of the idea, I think, is that humanity is something we possess not as separate individuals but as a collective. (The key idea would be, I think, that in some sense of the word 'human' a single individual could not be a human being any more than they could be a state, or a football team: humanity in this sense involves treating oneself and others as having a certain status.)

[4] This requirement seems to satisfied not just in cases of judicial punishments inflicted by states on their citizens but also in other cases where I think Duff would say that we rightly talk of punishment, such as punishments inflicted by religious bodies or academic institutions by their members, on children by their parents and so on: in each case we can see punishments as being determined by someone authorized to speak as the voice of the community.

Perhaps most importantly of all, none of these answers seem able to explain how tribunals constituted in the actual world – whether along the lines of an International Criminal Court, or along the more *ad hoc* lines of the Nuremberg Tribunals and the bodies that have dealt with war crimes in the former Yugoslavia – could acquire the right to speak on behalf of a universal moral community. By contrast one might hope that if we could establish that war criminals and their judges were members of a single political community, questions about how international tribunals could speak on behalf of those communities might seem more tractable.

If this is correct, it suggests that the kind of community we need in this context is not a moral community, but an international political community. The idea that there is such a community may initially seem somewhat far-fetched. There are two reasons why it is not. The first derives from considerations about what constitutes a political community, which go back as far as Aristotle. In book 1 of the *Politics*, Aristotle argues that it is a mark of political communities that they should be self-sufficient. It is not clear how Aristotle himself understood this idea: on his view Greek city states were examples of political communities, and yet Aristotle was presumably well aware that such communities engaged in foreign trade.[5] Still one might think there was a sense in which individuals who are, as a matter of fact, economically dependent on one another should be seen as members of a single community.[6] If so, then there is a good empirical case for thinking that there is a very large community which comprises very many of the world's inhabitants even if not all of them.

A further point is that insofar as different states enter into commercial relationships with one another or provide a home to economic entities which trade across national borders, there are certain forms of regulation that apply transnationally.[7] Thomas Pogge makes much of what one might see as the negative side of this point, namely that insofar as it makes sense to think in terms of there being a world economic order – which does not simply involve the existence of commercial relations between individuals or organizations in different parts of the world, but

---

[5] Aristotle *Politics* 1252b–1253a.

[6] We might still want to differ from Aristotle by recognizing that units which were economically interdependent might have smaller parts which could also be seen as communities in their own right, so that simple economic interdependence was a sufficient condition for the existence of a community, but not constitutive of the only form of community worth considering in this context.

[7] Aristotle *Politics* 1252b–1253a.

also the existence of a set of institutions and regulations governing these institutions – we have obligations of justice to those who are affected by them. However, another implication of this line of argument is that the existence of an institutional structure of this sort establishes that the individuals who are subject to it can be seen as members of a common community.

A third point is also worth mentioning. There seems to be an especially strong case for regarding the leaders of state and other state officials as being members of a world-wide community. Leaders of states occupy a position which is defined by a wide range of formal rules and informal conventions. These allow state leaders to act on behalf of their populations in the diplomatic sphere, to conclude economic arrangements which may be to the detriment of parts of their population, to make laws which criminalize parts of their population and so forth. Such conventions do not simply cease to exist in times of war; but even if they did, the fact that state leaders and their representatives have benefited from the existence of such rules seems to establish the existence of a community which goes wider than the nation state and of which they can reasonably be taken to be members.

3   The problem of non-state punishment

In Chapter 3 I argued that advocates of expressivist theories of punishment needed to say something about precisely whose attitudes were being expressed in standard case of punishment. I argued that in the paradigmatic case of punishment we could see punishment as expressing a collective judgment on the part of a political community. I also argued that if one is a member of such a society, one has reason to defer to the kind of judgment which punishment expresses, since it expresses a judgment made by a collective of which one is a member.

One might wonder whether this account can be extended to cover the punishment of war crimes. For one might think that it is essential that the kind of political community we are considering in this context should be a state. I have explicitly limited the subject matter of this book to legal punishment: punishment inflicted in response to the breach of a law. Someone who thinks that only states can make laws may infer that only states can inflict legal punishment, and that *a fortiori,* only states can inflict justified punishment. However, the claim that only states can make laws is apt to seem question-begging in the context of a debate such as this one. The issue of whether international law is genuinely a form of law is a vexed one, with authoritative figures coming down on both sides.[8] In the context of a debate over the punishment of war crimes it seems appropriate to assume that they can.

A more significant question is whether international tribunals can be seen as speaking on behalf of the kind of international community whose existence I argued for in Section 4. In order to address this question, it is worth considering how one might address a similar question in the case of domestic punishment. The question in this case would be: why should we regard the punishments inflicted by domestic courts as embodying the judgments of a domestic political community. A plausible answer would refer to two features of courts. The first, and most obvious, is that such courts express judgments in accordance with duly made law. To the extent that laws can be regarded as expressions of the will of a collective body, (as I suggested in Chapter 3), the enforcement of such laws on the part of courts can also be.

The second feature of courts, which is equally important in this context, is that such courts are constituted in the right kind of way: in accordance with the right kind of legally determined procedures. It is clear that although these procedures may vary from community to community, they play an important role in grounding the claim of a court to be giving expression to the views of any particular community: an *ad hoc* committee made up of self-selecting members of the public would not normally be regarded as having the right to express judgments on the part of the community via the imposition of penalties, even if their determinations of the legality or otherwise of certain forms of conduct were legally impeccable.

This suggests that an advocate of an expressivist account of the punishment of war crimes needs to address two issues. The first is whether, and to what extent, international law can be regarded as expressing the will of an international community, of which individuals who are charged with war crimes can be regarded as members. The second is whether international tribunals can be regarded as being constituted in the right kind of way as to make the sentences they impose count as judgments imposed by an international political community.

One might think that disanalogies between the ways in which domestic law comes into existence and the ways in which international law comes into existence make it difficult to give a positive answer to the first question. In democratic states, domestic law typically comes into existence as the result of legislation on the part of a representative body.

---

[8] Kelsen 1952; Hart 1983; Raz 1970; Vinx 2007. I am indebted to my colleague Lars Vinx for useful discussion and pointers to relevant literature here.

For this reason it seems plausible to regard it as involving a commitment to certain norms on the part of a collective body. But international law is not, typically, made in this way. Some international law depends on treaties. These can be regarded as expressing commitments by those nations that have signed those treaties. But it is arguable that at least some parts of international criminal law depend on customary law, and here the position seems much murkier.[9]

One might think that there is an analogy between the role of customary law in international law and common law in legal systems such as English law. However, this only postpones the question unless we can explain why the provisions of common law can be regarded as among the things which a political community is committed to collectively. One possible answer is that this is plausible to the extent to which common law provisions are capable of being overturned by statute. But the relationship between treaty-based law and customary law does not seem to be analogous to the relationship between customary law and statute-based law in this respect.

Here is an alternative suggestion. For something to be recognized as part of customary international law, it must pass two tests: universal practice and *opinio juris*. These two tests together ensure that something only counts as a part of customary international law if states conform to it because they take it to be the case that they are legally required to do so. But this means that something will only be part of international law if states take it to be the case that there is a collective commitment on the part of other states to act as though they are so committed, and are committed to act on that basis in the light of what they take to be a collective commitment. While it may be conceivable for a group to take it to be the case that a collective commitment exists in the absence of such a commitment, we should expect such cases to be rare: they are unlikely to escape the sort of public scrutiny that legal judgments, by their nature, are likely to attract. So we can take the existence of customary international law to pose less of a problem than we might here think.

It is less clear whether international criminal tribunals share the second feature of domestic courts to which I drew attention earlier: that of being constituted in a way that makes it clear that they are authorized to express and enforce the judgments of an international community. Many such tribunals are set up on an *ad hoc* basis, and as a result of political compromises of various kinds. There is also room to doubt whether

---

[9] May 2008.

those who instituted them have always intended that they should be effective in enforcing criminal norms.

One response to this would be to suggest that this demonstrates that *ad hoc* tribunals such as the International Criminal Tribunal for Rwanda (ICTR) and International Criminal Tribunal for the former Yugoslavia (ICTY) cannot legitimately speak for an international community and that only a more formally constituted body, such as the ICC, could do so. This would be a pessimistic conclusion, given the initial motivation of this chapter. A more optimistic conclusion might be supported by the following thought. The legal constitution of a court is a sufficient, rather than a necessary condition for taking it to speak on behalf a community. Bodies which are constituted in other, more *ad hoc*, ways may also be taken to speak on the part of a community on a defeasible basis. Their claim to speak in this way would be undermined if it were subjected to significant and sustained challenge from a wide range of members of the community; but in the absence of such widespread challenges, we may legitimately take them to do so.

4 Who is a member of the international community?

In Section 4 I argued for the existence of an international community. In Section 5 I argued that international judicial bodies can be regarded as speaking on behalf of such a body. But we also need to ask about the members of this international community, and in particular, whether the individuals on whom they pass sentence are members of that community.

It does not simply follow for the existence of an international political community that the members of such communities are individuals. Someone might, instead, suppose that the international community's members are states – that is to say – other collectives. However, I think we can argue that there is an international collective whose members are individuals. I argued in Section 4 that one reason for taking there to be a world-wide community that embraced both those who had committed war crimes and those who sought to punish them derived from the existence of conventions defining the position and role of state leaders. We might call the community which exists in virtue of these conventions 'the community of nations'.

Can this line of argument be extended to individuals below the level of state leaders with command responsibility? One might hope so, particularly in view of the difficulty – which Larry May has emphasized – in establishing the existence of *mens rea* in war crimes prosecutions of state leaders.[10] But whether or not it can seems to depend on two issues, neither of which seems straightforward. The first is the extent to which we can see the conventions which define the positions of state leaders as also covering individuals who are appointed to positions by them. In the case of many civilian officials, it seems easy to make this case: the powers and privileges of such individuals often depend on them having been appointed by recognized heads of state; and to the extent that they do so they thereby depend on the existence of conventions that relate to the recognition of heads of state. It seems less clear that this is the case with military leaders.

Once we reach the level of the common soldier, claims about their membership in the community of nations and claims that this member-ship can be seen as voluntary are apt to seem particularly problematic. So if we are interested in the possibility of a communicative justifica-tion of punishment we might want to look at other reasons for taking these individuals to be members of a world-wide community. (Such reasons, insofar as they apply to soldiers *as such* might also be expected to ground justifications of punishments for individuals with command responsibility below the level of state leaders other than their civilian appointees.)

There are two sorts of consideration that one might want to appeal to here. The first is based on considerations about the economic inter-dependence of individuals in separate nations. Call a community whose existence is based on such considerations 'the human commu-nity'. One might also want to claim that there are considerations other than economic ones that establish that soldiers in particular are members of a community that goes beyond a single nation. In partic-ular, one might hold that the existence of the sorts of norms which establish the existence of war crimes in the first case – what are some-times called the laws of war – establish the existence of a community of which they are members – what one might call the 'community of combatants'.

5   What is expressed?

We saw in Chapter 4 that advocates of a denunciatory theory of punish-ment need to explain why the expression of denunciatory messages via harsh treatment is justified. I argued there that if the expressive view is

---

[10] May 2007, chapter 12.

to seem plausible, then the sort of expression of disapproval that we are interested in must be one that is clearly sincere. And it is arguable that in at least some cases, the conduct of a society that allowed for public denunciations of criminal behavior but allowed those who engaged in it to do so without taking further action against them would not be seen in this way.[11]

However, one might also worry that the account of the punishment of war criminals that I have advanced here could be used to justify harsher treatment of war criminals than we are likely to think appropriate. If punishment is justified because it is a justifiable form of social disapproval of certain actions, why go to all the trouble and expense of actually *trying* war criminals? After all, in many cases their guilt is not in any real doubt. And in some cases it is arguable that war criminals derive unreasonable benefit from the states that try them being determined to go through the form of a fair trial.

To solve this problem I suggest that we go beyond the confines of an expressive view of punishment and consider the expressive role of the legal process.[12] An account of this sort will explain not just why we feel justified in inflicting harsh treatment on war criminals but also why we take it to be important that these punishments should be inflicted according to legal formulations – even when the legal standing of such tribunals is dubious.

What expressive role might international tribunals for war crimes fulfill? One answer might be that the purpose is the expression of disapproval of the actions that they are alleged to have committed. This is unsatisfactory. It may be painful to be subjected to legal proceedings. But we do not normally see this as a way of expressing disapproval of the alleged actions that the proceedings are about. We do not necessarily see it as a mark of societal disapproval when someone is subjected to civil legal proceedings.

A more satisfactory answer might be that the practice of subjecting war criminals to quasi-legal processes expresses a commitment to a certain

---

[11] Similar points have been made by Primoratz 1989, Narayan 1993 and Baldwin 1999.

[12] Expressive accounts of the trial have been developed by Duff 1986, 2007 and Duff et al. 2007. However, the account I give emphasizes different aspects of the trial. This should be unsurprising, given that international tribunals differ from domestic courts (on which Duff and his co-workers focus) in a number of important respects.

ideal of justice.[13] It is difficult to be precise about what the content of this ideal might be. But it is plausible that it might include at least the following ideas. The first is that the use of power by those that have it not be entirely unconstrained. The second is that that power should not be exercised in a way that gives no voice to those over whom it is exercised. This suggestion raises an important question – namely, why we should regard this as an ideal to which a society ought to express a public commitment. The second is whether, even granted that the expression of commitment to such an ideal is valuable, it can be invoked as a justification for trying war criminals.

Few reflective people would want to deny that the use of power should be constrained or that the constraints on its use should be ones that give a voice to those over whom it is exercised. To say this is to say that one sort of political freedom – the sort that involves independence from the arbitrary will of others – is widely acknowledged to be valuable. However, to say this is not yet to say that the public expression of such a commitment, and in particular its public expression through the judicial process, is valuable. Nevertheless, it is possible to construct an argument linking the two. One reason for thinking that this sort of independence from arbitrary wills is important is that it is good for the citizens of a state that power should be constrained in such a way. It is good not necessarily because it is what they prefer or because it is liable to make them happy, but because it is more likely to let them develop into virtuous citizens. On this view, one of the things that is most pernicious about dependence is the way in which it fosters certain kinds of vice – over cautiousness, secretiveness and so on.[14]

---

[13] 'Express a commitment to a certain ideal of justice' is intended to mean more in this context than just 'act in such a way as one would act if one were so committed.' On this minimalist reading of the word 'express', it is not clear what would be contributed to the defense of the practices of punishing war crimes by the suggestion that they express such a commitment. I take 'express a commitment' here to mean something like 'make a public declaration of a commitment'. Given this reading, it is a consequence of the expressivist account that it is important that trials are in some sense public events. It is not clear to me that this would be a consequence of my view on a more minimalist reading of 'express'. (I would like to thank an anonymous referee for *Law and Philosophy* for insisting on clarification here.)

[14] The general idea that institutions might be justified by considerations of the ways in which they affect people's character is an important insight from the civic republican tradition in political philosophy and political theory. But it is reasonable to ask what sort of evidence might be brought in favor of specific claims of this sort, like the one I am relying on here. Within the civic republican

If this is why such ideals are important then it is possible to see why the public expression of them is important as well. If independence from the arbitrary use of power is to be important in promoting the development of virtues, then it is important not only that people should in fact be independent in this kind of way but that they should be aware of so being. One way of making people more aware of this, and consequently less likely to be afraid of the possibility of dependence, is for a commitment to preventing the arbitrary use of power to be one that is publicly expressed not only by individual members of the society but also by its institutions.[15]

As I noted earlier, the sort of expressivism I have been defending in this chapter is not just a special case of a general expressivist justification of punishment. For it depends, in a way that those justifications did not, on a view about the expressive function of the trial. This point might be taken to vindicate the suspicion that there is something non-standard about the trial and punishment of war criminals. The account given suggests that the justification for trying and punishing war criminals

---

tradition, one sort of source of support has often been an appeal to historical examples – but this is unlikely to be helpful when we are considering proposals for new kinds of institution. Another possible source of support would be in empirical (social) psychology. Equally, though, empirical psychologists have a tradition of being skeptical about the very notion of character – and this has sometimes been thought to present problems for the relying on anything at all like the notion of a character trait in moral or political philosophy – though not always with very good reason. (See for example, Harman 1999 and Sreenivasan 2002 for, respectively, a well-known expression of a skeptical view, and a well-informed critique.) I suggest that the best way of defending a view like mine would involve relying on two sorts of claim: one about the effects of institutions on actual behavior (which ought to be susceptible of empirical investigation in a fairly straightforward manner), and one about the influence of habitual behavior on character – harder to investigate – though not for that reason deserving of being immediately dismissed – but far from novel, philosophically speaking. (For discussion by one illustrious advocate of such a view see Burnyeat 1980.)

[15] It may be that if this is the *only* way in which ideals of this sort are expressed, then citizens will be unlikely to make a connection between war crimes trials and the municipal situation. If so, then more may be needed to justify the practice of trying war criminals. The justification would work best in a society in which many institutions expressed the same ideals. However I am inclined to think that even in a society in which *no* other institutions expressed an ideal of this sort, there would be ways for individuals to make the relevant connection. One thing that is important in this context is that war crimes trials are high-profile, controversial, public events – precisely the sorts of events which are likely to make members of a society reflect on their significance.

is parasitic on the existence of good reasons for enforcing the rule of law in the more general case. If such justifications did not exist then it would be hard to see why we should regard an expression of the sort of commitment which (on the view I am defending) is embodied in our practice as being valuable.

We should also notice that this non-standard account provides us with its own way of responding to the 'harsh treatment' challenge of Chapter 4 in this special case. The harsh treatment challenge typically involves the observation that the practice is only one of a number of means by which the messages conveyed by punishment might be conveyed, some of which might be preferable on other grounds. This line of argument is not available here, since it is not clear that there are any other means of expressing the commitment with which we are concerned here which are not parasitic on engaging in the practice. The best way to express a commitment to the rule of law is to subject to it even those who might otherwise think that they were likely to escape it.

Still, someone might conceivably agree with what I have said about the expressive role of war crimes trials and yet suggest that this provides us with a justification for trying war criminals, but not for actually punishing them – in the sense of subjecting them to harsh treatment. However, it is not clear whether a view of this sort is coherent. It would be difficult to imagine a society which engaged in war crimes trials without following those up with the normal consequences of trials – in particular, with punishment for the guilty – as being sincere in its condemnation of the behavior of war criminals.

Considerations of proportionality seem to support these considerations of sincerity. It is generally accepted that for a system of punishments as a whole to be just, serious crimes should, on the whole, be punished more severely than less serious ones. On the assumption that if any crimes are serious, war crimes are, a system of punishment that allowed war criminals to be tried but not punished would involve gross violations of proportionality. This, if nothing else, would appear to give us reason to doubt the sincerity of the form of expression involved.

6   The 'Victor's Justice' problem

Many people believe that at least some war criminals should be punished. Cynicism and political expediency might lead some to dissent. However, some authors have suggested a more principled reason for disagreeing – namely, that punishments of war criminals typically involve 'Victor's

Justice' rather than real justice. The notion of Victor's Justice is a complex one.[16] However one aspect of it which will be significant for the purposes of this chapter is that in practice the trial and punishment of war criminals typically only involves the inflicting of harsh treatment on selected members of the losing side of a conflict rather than the application of impartial principles to combatants on both sides.[17] Thus, for example, we do not find the men who ordered the fire-bombing of Dresden standing trial alongside the Nazis at Nuremberg, even though these men's actions were as much in breach of the war crimes convention as those of the men who were responsible for Nazi atrocities in Occupied France.

In the light of this observation, one might think that justifications for punishing war crimes are undermined because they do not meet an intuitive constraint: that punishments should be inflicted for non-arbitrary reasons.[18] Since, in many cases, it is hard to regard the fact that someone ends up on the winning side rather than the losing side of a war as anything more than a matter of luck, and since it is reasonable to think that matters of luck should be irrelevant to how seriously one is punished for crimes that one has committed, it seems that the constraint might be violated in cases of Victor's Justice.[19]

Someone might deny that those who are in fact punished for war crimes are being punished for the wrong sorts of reasons. After all,

---

[16] Aspects of the notion of 'Victor's Justice' which I do not discuss include the question of whether punishing individuals for war crimes involves anything analogous to retrospective legislation and the issue of whether there are problems about punishing heads of states and other government officials for official acts. I am grateful to Efraim Podoksik and to an anonymous reader for helping me to disentangle several important issues here.

[17] In emphasizing this aspect of the notion of Victor's Justice I am following Wilkins 2001.

[18] Some might think that it derives from a conceptual requirement that for something to count as punishment it must be inflicted on non-arbitrary grounds. However I find appeals to supposed conceptual requirements of this sort unconvincing: see Hart 1959 for a fuller discussion.

[19] Arguably, luck can play a role in determining which offense an individual is guilty of: a lucky miss may turn someone who would otherwise have been a murderer into someone who is guilty of only attempted murder, and thus, in some circumstances make them liable for a lighter penalty. Some authors think that there is an injustice in allowing luck of this sort ('outcome luck') to play in determining what offense an individual has committed (see e.g. Ashworth 1988). But this is irrelevant for the present purposes. The point that I am making only concerns the role which luck should play in the treatment of two individuals who are guilty of the *same offense*.

those who are punished (we may assume) have indeed committed such crimes. Their having committed those crimes plays at least some role in explaining why they have been singled out for punishment: it is not as if the punishment is meted out indiscriminately to combatants on the losing side. Consider an apparently analogous case: that of the case of a criminal who is caught and punished for an ordinary crime for which detection rates are low. Such a criminal might argue that they were being punished not because they had committed a crime but because they had been unlucky enough to get caught. However, we would not normally consider this to be a reason for not punishing them.

There is a significant disanalogy between this sort of situation and the sort of situation to which the proponent of the Victor's Justice objection draws our attention. We can see this by thinking about the reasons why individuals who commit certain crimes are punished in the two cases. In the case of the individual who has committed a crime for which detection rates are low, the explanation does not involve anyone's deliberate agency: no-one has decided that those who don't get caught will be spared punishment.[20] It is simply an unfortunate fact that criminals who don't get caught cannot be punished. So although the fact that a criminal has been caught is part of the explanation of why he has been punished, the fact that criminals who are not caught go unpunished does not undermine the claim that the punishment is directed at the perpetrator of the crime for the right sorts of reasons.

However, where the differential prosecution of war crimes is concerned, agency is involved: there are particular individuals whose decisions determine that some types of individuals are tried and punished while others are not. So there is some reason for thinking that the points to which the proponents of the Victor's Justice objection draw our attention should undermine our confidence in thinking that the reasons for which the punishment is carried out are the right ones. (And we might say something similar about differential prosecution in the domestic case when this depends on decisions which are in the hands of prosecutors, rather than the simple impossibility of trying criminals who have not been caught.)

---

[20] Matters might be different if, for example, a general amnesty for undetected crimes of the sort in question were to be declared after a certain period of time. But it isn't beyond controversy that such an amnesty would involve no injustice to those that had been tried and punished – however difficult we might find it to extend our sympathy to such individuals in the case of some crimes.

7 Replying to the Victor's Justice objection: the public interest

Anthony Ellis is unimpressed by the Victor's Justice objection.[21] He suggests that although facts about disproportionate punishment might suggest that there is a *prima facie* case that people are being punished for morally irrelevant reasons, this case can be rebutted. For he holds that the *prima facie* case against punishing groups disproportionately can be over-ridden by considerations of public interest. As he points out, municipal law often gives prosecutors leeway on whether to proceed with prosecutions of crimes on public interest grounds and suggests that a similar 'public interest' criterion can be applied in the case of prosecutions for war crimes.[22]

Ellis thinks the operation of the same kind of public interest criterion can explain and justify the asymmetrical treatment given to those accused of war crimes on winning and losing sides. However, he says very little about why he takes the operation of public interest considerations in the domestic case to be defensible. However, in a subsequent account of why he takes war crimes punishments to be defensible he appeals to broadly consequentialist considerations. So I shall assume that he would suggest that the public interest considerations he appeals to here could be defended on similar lines.

One difficulty that any such defense appears to face is that it is very difficult to know what the consequences of this practice are and whether they are indeed beneficial. Does the policy deter individuals from committing atrocities, or does it make those who have done so more careful about covering up the evidence of their crimes, more tenacious in hanging on to power at any cost, and less likely to surrender when their military position is hopeless? It is difficult to know, and difficult to see how we could have reliable information on this topic.

The effects of war crimes trials on the conduct of individuals who are prosecuting wars is likely to depend a great deal on the circumstances of each particular war: the circumstances in which the war breaks out; the military culture of the opposing sides; the history of relations between combatants on both sides; the estimated chances of victory and consequences of defeat; and so on. It is also likely to be affected by the ways in which prosecutions for war crimes have operated on previous occasions – and how they have been seen as

---

[21] Ellis 2003.
[22] Ibid., pp. 101–2.

operating by the combatants. Assessing the effects that these are likely to have in particular cases is something that might be possible – but probably not until a considerable time after they have taken place. By contrast, the consequentialist needs a way of judging how the prospect of war crimes trials is likely to affect combatants in wars which have not yet taken place.

We might think that considerations of equal treatment might override public interest considerations in at least some cases. This claim is intuitively plausible. However a committed consequentialist might respond that the intuition is simply misleading. Nevertheless these intuitions can be backed up by considerations to which someone with consequentialist leanings ought to be sympathetic.[23] For example, differential treatment of different groups justified along the lines suggested above is likely to lead to contempt for the law, both on the part of those who are treated leniently (since they may be inclined to notice and exploit their relative impunity) and those who are treated more harshly (since they are likely to become cynical). And contempt for the law may well lead to that law being more frequently disregarded.[24]

Here, we are confronted by a situation in which a general rule (to the effect that prosecutorial discretion on grounds of public interest should be disallowed) can be defended by reference to its consequences, but comes into conflict with a less general rule (to the effect that prosecutorial discretion can be allowed in the case of some types of trial but not of others), which can also be defended by reference to its consequences. A defender of Ellis' position needs to suggest and argue for an appropriate procedure for deciding what the appropriate level of generality for such rules to operate at might be. He or she also needs to show that this procedure will deliver the sort of answer he needs. It is far from obvious that either can be done. So I conclude that Ellis's appeal to public interest considerations to defeat the Victor's Justice objection fails.

---

[23] I take the moral intuition that a legal system that operated like this would be *deserving* of contempt to be a compelling one, without the consequentialist backing that I give it. But for the reasons I note, this point will be unhelpful in arguing against the consequentialist.

[24] Notice that it doesn't help the consequentialist to object that the defense of the intuition relies on implausible story-telling. They are in no position to make the complaint, since his or her own position seems to rely on similar story-telling.

8 Victor's Justice revisited

Fortunately the denunciatory version of expressivism which I have defended here enables us to meet the Victor's Justice objection in a different way. We should start by observing that the fact that a form of punishment is applied disproportionately to a particular group does not by itself undermine its expressive function. So, if the justification of a form of punishment depends on this expressive function, this fact does not undermine its justification. This is an instance of a more general truth about expression. Furthermore, endorsement of the expressive account does not, on its own, commit someone to any independent general moral principles that might underpin a version of the objection. In this respect it is markedly different from the consequentialist accounts which I considered earlier.

However one might think that the expressivist account contains some elements that make it capable of generating a version of the Victor's Justice objection. For example, one might ask whether, in view of the facts to which the Victor's Justice objection draws our attention, we really can see the practice of punishing war criminals as expressive of a commitment to ideals of justice, rather than of a commitment to revenge. This point can be rebutted by observing that the practice of punishing war criminals is expressive of a commitment to justice rather than revenge to the extent that the punishment is only handed out at the end of a process that follows juridical norms as closely as possible. An attractive consequence of this view is that it explains why it is important that war criminals should be tried as well as punished, even in cases where it seems beyond reasonable doubt that they are guilty.

One might also press the Victor's Justice objection by suggesting that a system of trying and punishing war criminals should express a commitment to the principle of treating like cases alike and that the facts that the proponent of the Victor's Justice objection points to suggest that it does no such thing. One response would be to deny that a legal system should embody a commitment of this sort. However, this seems implausible. For it seems as though the requirement that like cases should be treated alike is a basic requirement of procedural justice, and as such one which any system of trial and punishment should express.

A more plausible response would involve accepting that there is a good case for thinking that a legal system should express an ideal of procedural justice; and then noting that in this case (at least if the objector is right) the requirement to express a commitment to procedural justice comes into conflict with other things that we might legitimately expect from our system of trial and punishment. If so, we need some account of how we might rank the different sorts of ideals which we might legitimately expect our penal regime to give expression to in cases of conflict.

The rationale which I gave earlier for wanting our legal system to express a commitment to preventing the arbitrary use of force seems to provide an answer in this particular case. I argued that a good reason for wanting our penal system to express such a commitment was because of the long-term effects that the fear of dependence can have on the development of the character of individuals. It is not so obvious that an unbending commitment to an ideal of procedural justice is significant in the same way. Indeed, one might suspect that the expression of such a commitment under all circumstances would be deleterious rather than beneficial to the development of individuals – for example by teaching them that the legal system is liable to be inflexible.

7
Punishing Corporations

1 Introduction

In the course of the last two chapters we have seen how a denunciatory account of punishment can help to make sense of some kinds of non-paradigmatic instance of punishment. However, the kinds of case we have looked at have had something in common with paradigmatic instances of punishment. For they have been, in each case, examples of the punishment of individuals. In the next two chapters, I wish to look at instances of punishment which differ from the paradigmatic case in another respect: the punishment of collective agents. In this chapter I shall focus on what one might call the 'domestic' case: the punishment of corporations under domestic law; in the next chapter I shall focus on something which one might take to be considerably more problematic: the punishability of states under international law.

One reason for treating the domestic case first is that many jurisdictions do, on occasion, appear to treat collective entities as appropriate subjects of punishment.[1] Two things follow from this. The first is that we should not regard it as a counter-intuitive consequence of a theory of punishment that it entails those corporate entities can be punished.165 Of course, we should not regard it as a requirement on the acceptability

---

[1] For further detail see Wells (2001) who writes: 'From the common law point of view, it is clear that criminal law does address non-human (i.e. corporate) agents, albeit in a somewhat reluctant and sometimes obscure way' (Wells 2001, p. 147). As she notes (p. 138), this has traditionally not been true of civil law jurisdictions, although this too is changing: for example, in 1991 the French penal code was altered to remove a principle that criminal liability could not attach to 'personnes morales' (Jeandidier 1991 p. 341 cited in Wells 2001 p. 139).

of a theory of punishment that it should vindicate every feature of contemporary judicial practice. But the fact a theory does vindicate such practice should, on the whole, be regarded as a point in its favor rather than a point against it.

By the same token the fact some jurisdictions do treat corporate entities as being liable to punishment makes it reasonable to expect a theory of punishment to cast some light on the reasons we might have for doing so. While it need not necessarily count as a compelling argument against a theory of punishment that it entails that corporate entities cannot be punished, it seems reasonable to think that it counts against it to some extent: we might expect someone whose theory entails that corporate entities cannot be punished to explain why, in that case, they are treated under some jurisdictions as entities that can be punished.

I shall argue that denunciatory versions of expressivism can make much better sense of the practice of punishing corporations than communicative views can. One might take this as an argument additional to those put forward in Chapters 3 and 4 for preferring a denunciatory version of an expressive view to a communicative one across the board. For an account of this sort will permit one to put forward a unified theory of punishment. However, someone who does not accept these arguments might, nevertheless, want to accept the conclusions of this chapter. In other words, someone might accept a communicative version of expressivism in the individual case, but prefer a denunciatory account of the punishment of corporations. For, as I shall argue in what follows, communicative theories face particular difficulties in accounting for the punishment of collective entities.

2   Can corporations be punished? non-expressive considerations

For the purposes of this paper, I shall take it for granted that under many circumstances it is legitimate to treat business corporations as collective agents. There is a large philosophical literature arguing in favor of this view, and I have little to add to it.[2] However, it does not follow from the fact that we regard business corporations as collective agents that we have to see them as the kind of entities which are, in principle, capable of undergoing punishment. For it might follow from our understanding

---

[2] French 1984; List and Pettit 2011.

of the nature of punishment that corporations are simply not the kind of thing which can be punished.[3]

As we saw in earlier chapters, non-expressive theories of punishment typically specify that punishment involves: (1) harsh treatment directed at an agent by (2) an appropriate official (3) in response to a breach of a law. I have argued further (in Chapter 2) that harsh treatment can only constitute punishment if (4) it is imposed in pursuit of the right kinds of expressive goals.[4] I shall take it for granted that the lawful imposition of sanctions such as monetary fines on corporate bodies can satisfy conditions (2) and (3). Matters are less obvious with conditions (1) and (4), the 'harsh treatment' and 'expressive' considerations.

Many authors take punishment to be harsh treatment which is aimed at causing pain or suffering. If we understand the notion of harsh treatment in this way, it will be hard to see how states can be punished. Only conscious beings can experience pain or suffer. Since states are not conscious they cannot – except metaphorically – experience pain or suffer. If so, they cannot be subject to harsh treatment. Consequently, they cannot be punished. In Chapter 2, I argued that harsh treatment should not be understood as punishment which is aimed at causing suffering, but as treatment of a kind which is likely to cause an offender of a particular type to suffer. However, since business corporations are not the kinds of agent which can suffer, this account also entails that we cannot inflict harsh treatment on business corporations or punish them.

However, if we think of business corporations as agents, we can also think of them as having interests. The interests of a business corporation are typically related to the interests of its employers, directors and shareholders in a somewhat indirect manner. It can be in the interests of the corporation that certain employers or directors be sacked, even if this is very much against their interests. And there may be cases where the interests of a corporation conflict with the interests of its shareholders: consider a case where individuals who are being negatively impacted by a corporation's activities each buy a share in the corporation in order to engage in some sort of protest.

Can the interests of a corporation conflict with the interests of all of its shareholders? I think that they can: we might argue that it is in

---

[3] I am indebted to Sylvia Rich (personal communication) for emphasizing the importance of this issue.

[4] In Wringe 2010 I also argue that the 'appropriate official' condition is only satisfied if the harsh treatment with the right kind of expressive goals is imposed by those who are in a position to speak on behalf of a community whose laws have been violated.

everyone's interest, including that of the shareholders of fossil-fuel companies, to prevent catastrophic climate change. It might neverthe-less be the case that the only action that we can realistically take that would prevent such climate change would be to bring the existence of certain corporations to an end. In a case like this it seems plausible that what was in the interest of the corporation would conflict with what was in the interest of all of the shareholders.)

How, then, might we identify the interests of a business corporation? One way of doing so would be to start from considerations of what it is for such an organization to flourish. Corporate entities are typically set up with certain ends in view. These ends may be specified in the articles of association for the corporation (in the case of bodies incorporated under the law of specific jurisdictions); or they may be specified more informally. They may – and often will – include the purpose of providing profit for shareholders; but we can also consider, along analogous lines, the cases of collective entities which are established with some other end in view (e.g., the provision of charitable relief). We can then think of the interests of the organization as being conditions whose fulfill-ment makes possible, or facilitates, the corporation's pursuit of these ends through its corporate activities.

This way of understanding the notion of corporate interests gives us a way of giving content to the idea of a corporate entity being treated harshly.[5] We can say that a corporate entity has been treated harshly if measures have been imposed on it which would foreseeably damage its interests, or which would foreseeably damage the interests of similar corporate entities. Among the kinds of measure that might satisfy this condition are large monetary fines; exclusion of a corporation from oper-ating in certain markets or certain areas; the disbarment or the imposi-tion of sanctions on employees or directors (but only to the extent that these were seen as impacting on the ability of the corporation to achieve its ends) and, in extreme cases, the dissolution of the corporation.

Someone might object that the conception of harsh treatment which I have outlined here is too dissimilar from the conception which I outlined for paradigmatic cases of punishment in Chapter 2 for it to be anything other than misleading to use the same word in both cases. I disagree. There is a clear analogy between this notion of harshness and the one which I have used in the individual case. Even if the imposition of harsh treatment on corporate bodies does not involve the imposition

---

[5] This move was suggested to me by Avia Pasternak, 'Justifying the Punishment of States' (unpublished ms.). I have also benefitted from discussion of this issue with Sylvia Rich, although she would not accept the position I sketch here.

of suffering (as it does in the individual case), the effects of imposing treatment of the sort I have characterized as harsh on corporations is likely to be similar to the effect of imposing what I have characterized as harsh treatment on individuals. For it seems plausible to think that the kinds of measures which we take when we punish individuals are typically ones which frustrate their agency; and it is their capacity to frustrate agency, rather than simply the fact that they impose suffering, that makes them suitable as forms of punishment.

3   Expressive theories of corporate punishment

I have argued that we can treat corporations in ways which satisfy the non-expressive conditions on punishment. It may seem fairly straightforward to show that they can also satisfy the expressive conditions. For it might seem obvious that we will be able to express the same kinds of things by imposing harsh treatment on corporate entities as we can by imposing harsh treatment on individuals.

I think this conclusion is, broadly speaking, correct. However, there are two complications that are worth considering. We saw in Part I that there are a number of different forms which an expressive theory of punishment might take. I argued there that we had good reasons for preferring denunciatory accounts of punishment to communicative accounts and audience-independent accounts. However, it is not clear that all of the reasons that I gave for preferring denunciatory accounts to other kinds of expressive accounts in the individual case will carry over to the collective case. For example, I argued in Chapter 4 that in view of the risks of shaming and stigmatization which the public nature of punishment brings in its wake, it was incumbent on both communicative theorists and audience-independent theorists to provide some kind of rationale for punishment's having a public nature. But it is not clear that this line of argument can be carried over to the corporate case, since it is not clear that the shaming and stigmatization of corporate entities brings the same costs in its wake.

Similarly, it is not clear that the problem of harsh treatment arises for collective bodies in the same way that it does for individuals. For it is simply not clear that the fact that a course of action will harm the interests of a corporate body provides a *prima facie* reason not to engage in that course of action in the same way that inflicting suffering on an individual provides a *prima facie* reason for not engaging in that course of action. It is true, of course, that in many cases harming the interests of a corporate body will involve harming some particular individuals, but as we saw in Section 2 this need not always be the case. But in any case, in many situations any harms which individuals suffer when the interests of corporate bodies are harmed will be inflicted in rather indirect ways. The significance of this fact will emerge in due course.

Similarly, we cannot simply assume that the reasons I gave in Part I for thinking that a denunciatory account of the punishment of individuals does not involve treating them in ways which are impermissible can be straightforwardly transferred to the collective case. In particular, I argued in Chapter 4 that the denunciatory punishment of individuals does not involve impermissibly treating them as a mere means. The question of whether the punishment of collective bodies involves treating those bodies as a mere means might seem uninteresting, since it is far from obvious that there is anything morally problematic about treating collectives as a means.[6] But it might nevertheless turn out that the denunciatory punishment of corporate entities involves treating individuals as mere means. If so, it would be impermissible in a way that the denunciatory punishment of individuals would not be.

4   Communicative theories of corporate punishment: the intelligibility problem

According to Anthony Duff the justification of the harsh treatment which punishment involves depends essentially on the idea that punishment has a communicative function, and more particularly on the details of the communicative function it is supposed to have.[7] As we saw in Chapter 4, Duff takes punishment to involve harsh treatment directed at a member of a particular community with the goal of communicating societal disapproval of their norm-infringing behavior, to the end of inducing remorse or regret for that behavior.[8]

---

[6] For further discussion of this issue, see Wringe 2014.

[7] Duff 2001. Note that the claim is that the communicative function of punishment is essential to the *justification* of punishment: Duff appears to leave it open that there might be cases of punishment which do not have this function, although such cases of punishment would not be justified (or at least not in the standard way). See Duff 2001 pp. xiv–xv. (I thank an anonymous reader for impressing on me the need to emphasize this point.)

[8] It does not seem to be essential to Duff's view that harsh treatment should be inflicted with the intention of inflicting suffering. For this reason I believe that Duff's view escapes the objections of Hanna 2008. What makes the treatment 'harsh' is the fact that it is of a sort which would typically involve hardship on the part of those who are suitably similar to those on whom it is inflicted. See Wringe (under review) for further discussion.

It is not obvious how a communicative theory of punishment might be extended to cover the case of punishments inflicted on collective entities of this sort. Indeed, there are two problems that need to be faced. One arises from the fact that on Duff's view, punishment should be aimed at inducing regret or remorse. The second is that for the account to succeed in providing a justification of punishment, we must have some reasons for finding the remorse or regret which the punished individual experiences as having some kind of value. Call these two problems the 'Intelligibility of Collective Regret and Remorse Problem' and the 'Value of Collective Regret and Remorse Problem' – or the 'Intelligibility Problem' and 'Value Problem' respectively. I shall argue that although the Intelligibility Problem can be solved, the Value Problem cannot.

Someone might think that the main difficulty in showing how a communicative theory of punishment could be applied to the collective case is that it makes no sense to think of collectives experiencing regret or remorse. However, I shall argue that this is not the main problem that the communicative theorist faces. There are ways of understanding the ascription of emotions to collectives in ways that would suit the communicative theorist's purpose.

Someone who regards corporate bodies as possible objects of punishment is likely to regard such bodies as collective agents. Talk of collective agents may bring in its wake talk of collective beliefs and desires. Still, there seems to be a large gap between regarding collective bodies as *agents*, and regarding them as *subjects of experience*. One might hold that if we want to attribute emotions such as regret and remorse to collective bodies, we must regard them as subjects of experience and not just as agents; and that although they can be the latter they cannot be the former.

This objection might be thought to arise from a commitment to a mistaken model of emotion. Someone who accepts a 'judgmentalist' theory of emotion – of the sort put forward by Martha Nussbaum[9] – might reject the idea that it makes sense to think of collective bodies as being capable of having beliefs or desires but not as being subject to guilt or remorse. For if emotions involve a complex range of judgments, but no non-judgmental elements, there need be no obvious logical bar to thinking of collective bodies as subjects of emotions.

Many philosophers of emotion think that Nussbaum's judgmentalist account gives an inadequate account of emotional experience.[10]

---

[9] Nussbaum 1996 p. 168, 2001 p. 22.
[10] See for example Roberts 1999 pp. 797–8; Wringe (2015).

However, even if we accept Nussbaum's account, the possibility of collective emotions does not follow straightforwardly from the possibility of collective beliefs and judgments. In order to account for the phenomenology of many emotional states, Nussbaum appeals to features of the functional role of certain types of judgment – features relating to their 'freshness' and to their centrality to the identity of a subject. It is not clear that these can be replicated by any form of collective judgment.

The communicative theorist might instead suggest that we think of punishment as being aimed at inducing remorse in the individuals that act on behalf of a corporate body rather than in the corporate body itself. This response is unsatisfactory: it overlooks the fact that artificial persons can continue in existence while those who act on their behalf change. If the punishment of artificial persons was aimed at inducing remorse in the individuals who make up a corporate body, then in cases like this, it would be unjust: it would involve inflicting suffering on individuals who had not done anything to deserve it.

One might respond to this argument by suggesting that in cases where the membership of a collective body changes, it should be exempt from punishment. However this suggestion seems like a bad one: it would make it possible for corporations to avoid punishment too easily, since they could easily vote someone new on to the board; and it would appear to rule out the possibility of nations being punished at all, since their membership changes almost every second. One might also respond by arguing there is a logical bar to an individual's feeling remorse for acts committed by a collective body before they were a member of it or in a position to act on behalf of it. However, there seems to be little reason to think that such a logical bar exists.[11] Whether or not it is psychologically possible for an individual to feel remorse in a case like this will depend, in any given case, on the make-up of the individual and in particular how strongly they identify with the collective body of which they are a part.[12]

---

[11] There are some logical bars to what one can feel remorse for: elsewhere I have argued that one cannot feel remorse for actions that lie in the future. It may also be logically impossible to feel remorse for actions in cases where one has no connection of any sort with the agent. But in the case under consideration, one does have such a connection. What is in dispute between me and someone who thinks that in these cases remorse is logically impossible is whether the connection is of the right sort.

[12] I am grateful to an anonymous reader for forcing me to clarify the dialectical structure of this paragraph.

Margaret Gilbert makes a more promising suggestion.[13] Gilbert holds that groups can be the subjects of collective emotions, including the emotion of remorse. Collective emotions of this sort require group-members to have what she calls a 'joint commitment' to a particular emotional response on the part of the collective that they make up:

A group G feels remorse over an act A if and only if the members of A are committed to feeling remorse as a body over A. (Gilbert 2001 p. 229)

Gilbert does not gloss the phrase 'feeling remorse as a body' directly. However, she holds that a joint commitment to feeling remorse 'as a body' need not entail a commitment on the part of each individual in the group to feeling remorse on their own behalf:

I might be able correctly to avow 'we feel remorse over our act' without being able correctly to avow 'I feel remorse over our act'. (ibid.)

Gilbert does tell us what it is for a group to accept a goal as a body:

For two [or more – my addition] people to accept a goal as a body is for them *as far as is possible* to constitute through their several actions a single 'body' or person who accepts that goal. (ibid. p. 224; italics in original.)

However, it is not clear how much this helps. Even if it is possible for a group of individuals to act together in such a way as to constitute a body trying to achieve a certain goal, one might think that it is not possible for them to constitute a body which feels a certain way, on the grounds that only subjects of experience can have feelings, and that collective bodies are not subjects of experience.

However, even if collective bodies are not centers of experience in their own right, they can act in ways which correspond to the behavioral expressions of emotion. There are logical ties between remorse and its expression, and between sincere regret and the desire to make amends where appropriate. Where collective bodies have acted wrongly they can act collectively, in ways which if performed by an individual in response to individual wrongdoing, would constitute expressions of

---

[13] Gilbert 2001.

these emotions. For example the official spokesperson for a group can express regret for wrongdoing on behalf of a collective; collective bodies can look for and find ways of proceeding that prevent similar wrongs from happening in future; and they can act in ways that compensate those who have been harmed. We might see actions of this sort as behavioral analogues of remorse and regret; and a joint commitment to acting in these sorts of ways might be taken to constitute a joint commitment to *feeling* remorse *as a body*;[14] or alternatively, as an appropriate substitute for it in the collective case.[15] If so, then the fact that collectives are not subjects of experience need not present an insuperable problem to the advocate of the communicative view.

One might object that collective remorse, if conceived of in this way, seems like the remorse of an insincere individual, and the communicative theorist cannot give us any reason for valuing insincere remorse.[16] The objection fails: even if it is true that the communicative theorist should only care about sincere remorse, this presents no obstacle to the communicatively justified punishment of collectives. We can distinguish between sincere and insincere remorse in the case of collectives, just as we can in the case of individuals. Remorse is insincere if there is a mismatch between its verbal expressions and other typical behavioral expressions, such as attempts at reform. A collective's expressions of remorse may be insincere when not backed up by attempts to make amends where possible, just as an individual's can. They can also be sincere when they are so backed up. (In the case of an individual the reasons for which they are acting are relevant to whether their expression of a given emotion is sincere. The same will often be true where

---

[14] This suggestion is intended as sympathetic exegesis of Gilbert's position. But whether or not it is correct as exegesis, I take it to be a defensible view in its own right.

[15] I take it that in order to defend the application of the communicative view to collective bodies, it needs to be possible to say – as Gilbert does – that the collective body feels remorse, and not simply that it behaves remorsefully or (as one anonymous reader put it) acts in ways that express a belief on the part of its members that its behavior was defective (though if the collective body feels remorse, it will presumably do so in virtue of doing things like this): for further discussion, see the discussion of sincerity in subsequent paragraphs. Notice that this latter, apparently more cautious formulation does not, as one might think, avoid any commitment to a Gilbert-like 'plural subject': for the amended account to be at all plausible, the belief expressed must be some kind of a *collective* belief, rather than a belief held by each individual member of the collective body.

[16] I am grateful to Adam Morton for raising this point in correspondence.

corporations are concerned.[17] But the reasons for which corporations are acting are often best judged by reference to their behavior.)

5 The value of collective remorse

Even if it makes sense to talk of collective emotions, the communicative theorist faces another problem. This is that it is not clear that we should value remorse on the part of collective wrong-doers in the same way as we value the remorse of individual wrong-doers.

The justification of punishment that the communicative theorist puts forward can only function as a justification if one thinks that there is something good about agents who have committed crimes experiencing remorse or regret. As far as the punishment of individuals is concerned, there seems little difficulty here. For one might take this regret or remorse to be good in a number of ways. One might, for example, take it to be non-instrumentally valuable for individuals to have a proper appreciation of the moral quality of their action. Or one might think that this appreciation was a necessary part of the individual in question either having, or deserving, full moral standing in the community of which they are a member. Or, on a more mundane level, one might think that the experience of regret and/or remorse might have an effect on the character of an individual that would make them less likely to offend in future. Or one might appeal to a combination of all of these factors.

It is much harder to see how or why the behavioral analogue of regret or remorse in a collective body should be valuable. Even someone who is relaxed about allowing collectives into their metaphysics might well balk at regarding the mental states of collective entities as non-instrumentally valuable. And it is not clear whether we should see collectives as being part of our community in the way in which the individuals who make up that community presumably are.

One possibility to consider is that inducing the behavioral analogue of remorse in collective criminals might be good for at least some of the surviving victims of crimes, or for those who, while not being direct victims, have been harmed by the commission of the crimes. It certainly seems plausible that expressions of remorse by collective bodies which have harmed individuals might be of benefit to victims in some cases. For example, one might think that it is appropriate for the government of the USA to express regret or remorse over laws permitting slavery and

---

[17] I am grateful to Christopher Bennett for making this suggestion in correspondence.

racial segregation; and one reason for thinking this is appropriate might be that some form of limited acknowledgment of ways in which these laws have contributed to ongoing harms which have affected Black citizens of the USA up until the present day would be of some symbolic benefit to those who suffer those harms.[18]

However, this point is unlikely to contribute much to a defense of a communicative theory of punishment applied to collective bodies for two reasons. First, many corporate crimes involve inchoate offenses, such as recklessness.[19] Offenses of this sort often do not involve particularized harms to specifiable individuals. So a defense of the punishment of collectives which relies on the value of expressions of remorse and regret to such individuals is unlikely to cover all the kinds of cases where we might think that it is appropriate to punish collective entities. A second point is that in cases where expressions of remorse might be of value to victims, a significant part of whatever value they might have seems to be dependent on their being, and being seen as, freely given rather than coerced.[20]

One further possibility to consider is that collectives that act in ways which manifest the behavioral analogues of remorse and regret might be less likely to infringe the norms which had led to them being punished in the first place than they might be if they were not so punished. It is not clear whether this is true: it certainly seems open to doubt. Even if it were not, one might think that the advocate of the communicative view should be embarrassed by needing to rely on this point. For it seems to involve thinking that the purpose of punishing collective entities is simply to reduce the rate of corporate crime. But if one does think this, then it is hard to see why one should prefer a way of doing this which operates via the agency of particular corporate bodies to one that works through a wider variety of agencies, as, for example, a deterrent-based account might. If so, the communicative account seems otiose.

---

[18] This point was suggested to me by Copp (2010). Of course, in the case that Copp is considering, those most directly harmed by the actions in question are long dead, and cannot benefit from expressions of remorse, even though others can. We might hope that not all cases of corporate punishment would involve punishments being inflicted after the death of the victims.

[19] Wells 2001 pp. 5–6, 64.

[20] Does this point present a problem for the communicative theory as applied to individuals? No, because in the individual case the communicative theorist does not see the remorse suffered by the criminal in cases of effective punishment as being worthwhile because it benefits the victim of the crime.

6   Denunciatory theories of corporate punishment

I have argued that a communicative account of punishment like Duff's cannot shed any light on the punishment of corporate bodies. I shall now argue that denunciatory accounts, like the one which I defended in the first half of this book, do not face the same problems. On a denunciatory account, the intended audience of the message that punishment is supposed to communicate is not the perpetrator but the society whose norms have been transgressed. The content of the message would be that the society has certain norms and takes them seriously.

It is worth both noticing the initial plausibility of the claim that denunciatory communication of this sort might serve a valuable and social role; and also drawing attention to the fact that there is a range of benefits which one might appeal to in this context. In some of them, the role of the denunciation might be purely instrumental: for example, it might turn out that denunciation via punishment led to better corporate compliance. But other benefits might be less easily conceived of in ways which make them independent of the denunciatory message.[21] For example, one might think that citizens are benefited directly by living in a society which makes clear that collectives are just as subject to legal and moral assessment as individuals. This might, for example, contribute to a liberal society's goal of showing respect for the agency of its citizens, or of demonstrating a commitment to treating those with and those without powerful associates as equals.

One objection which is sometimes made to denunciatory accounts of the punishment of individuals is that such accounts appear to involve treating the punished individual merely as a means to an end: in this case, the end of a society communicating its norms to its members.[22] I argued in Chapter 4 that this objection could not be sustained against denunciatory theories of the punishment of individuals. However, as I argued in Section 4 of this chapter, it is not obvious that the kinds of consideration which I appealed to in that context can be apply to the punishment of collectives. For those considerations seemed to depend on the fact that individuals who are being punished are members of the political community that is punishing them. But corporations are not

---

[21] The fact that at least some of these goods are not identifiable independently of the practice means that this does not collapse into a consequentialist account. Cf. Duff 2001 p. 3; Michael 1992.

[22] Duff 2001.

members of a political community in the way that individuals are. So the same line of argument cannot apply to them.

A further limitation of the arguments of Chapter 4 in the present context is that they were aimed only at showing that the denunciatory punishment of offenders does not impermissibly treat offenders as a means. But one might think there is a further worry to address when we are concerned with the denunciatory punishment of collectives. This is that such punishment might impermissibly treat the members of such collectives as a means. Indeed one might worry that it does so precisely because it treats the collective as a means. In the remainder of this chapter I shall argue that considerations of treating agents as means do not provide an insuperable obstacle to imposing punishments with a denunciatory rationale on collective agents.

I shall not contest the claim that such punishments might involve treating collective agents as means (although it is far from clear to me that this is correct). Instead, I shall argue that even if they do so, this does not make them impermissible. My argument will have two main strands to it. First I shall argue that we are under no obligation not to treat collective agents as mere means other than obligations that might derive from our obligation not to treat individuals as means. Secondly I shall argue that even if punishments that have a denunciatory rationale might treat collective agents as a mere means, they do not involve treating individuals as mere means. This is because treating a collective as a mere means need not involve treating the individuals who form part of it as mere means.

7 What is it to treat someone as a mere means?

Before going any further, it will be helpful to examine more closely the claim that denunciatory punishment might involve treating either a collective agent or the individuals who make up that agent as a means. As Duff points out, the precise import of this Kantian language is far from clear.[23] There are at least three ways in which the prohibition might be understood. First, one might take it that an individual is treated as a mere means if they are treated in ways they have not actually consented to being treated in. However, it is arguable that on this view all accounts of punishment entail that punishment involves treating someone as a means. There is no plausible account of punishment that takes it only

---

[23] Duff 2001 p. 19.

to be justified in cases where individuals actually consent to it.[24] To put matters differently: if there is a prohibition on treating individuals in ways that they have not actually consented to, this constitutes an objection to punishment in any of the forms that it is currently conceived of, and not simply to the denunciatory account of the justification of punishment of collective agents which I am advocating here.

There are two other ways of understanding the prohibition that may be more worth considering. One is based on Duff's own interpretation of what the Kantian prohibition amounts to. He suggests that the Kantian prohibition on treating individuals as means should be equated with a requirement to treat individuals as persons or as responsible agents.[25] The other interpretation of the prohibition on treating individuals as mere means to an end can be found in Onora O'Neill's interpretation of Kant's moral philosophy. On O'Neill's account, an agent treats a second agent as a mere means when the first agent has as the maxim of their action something to which the second agent could not consent.[26]

These two interpretations of the prohibition on treating as mere means give rise to four ways in which punishments with a denunciatory rationale might wrongly treat some agent as a means. They might do so because they wrongly fail to treat a collective agent as a responsible agent; or because they wrongly fail to treat one or more individuals as responsible agents; or because they involve wrongly treating a collective on the basis of a maxim that it could not in principle consent to; or because they wrongly treat one or more individuals on the basis of a maxim they could not in principle consent to.

It is worth noticing that both of these accounts seem to entail that it is unlikely that punishments with a denunciatory rationale would involve treating individual members of a corporation as a mere means without treating the corporation itself as a mere means. On Duff's account this will be because insofar as individual members of the corporation are affected by denunciatory punishments imposed on a corporation, it will

---

[24] One might argue that by living in a particular territory, individuals consent both to the laws that govern them and the forms of punishment that are typically inflicted on them. If such an account was workable, (which I do not think likely) it would be true that the legal punishment of individuals does not involve treating people in ways in which they have not consented to being treated. But such individuals could presumably also be taken to have consented to laws governing corporate misbehavior. So on this account the denunciatory view is no worse than Duff's communicative account.

[25] Duff 2001 pp. 13–14.

[26] O'Neill 1989 pp. 110–7; Cf. Korsgaard 1996 pp. 137–40.

be the corporation rather than the individual at whom the denunciation is aimed. On O'Neill's account it is because it is hard to see why an individual affected by a denunciatory punishment would be unable, in principle, to consent to a collective of which they were a member being treated in a particular way.

8   May we treat collectives as means?

Let us consider the possibility that punishments of collectives which have a denunciatory rationale are wrong because they involve wrongly treating a collective as a means (whether we understand that along Duff's lines or O'Neill's). One natural response is that there is no case to answer, since there is no plausible general moral prohibition on treating such bodies as a mere means. Indeed one might think it was strange to treat them as anything else. However, one might wonder whether, in conceding that corporations are capable of remorse, I have already conceded that they are deserving of the kind of respect that makes it impermissible to treat them as means to an end.[27]

The suggestion here would be that a collective's being capable of remorse entails its seeing itself as a morally considerable agent; and that nothing – or at least very little – over and above being able to see oneself as a morally considerable agent – is required for one actually to be an agent who cannot permissibly be treated as a means to an end This line of argument is certainly ingenious. The conclusion, however, seems extremely implausible. So my aim will be to show that we can reject the claim that collective agents cannot permissibly be treated as a means to an end without needing to deny that they are capable of remorse.

Since the argument under discussion is framed in Kantian terms, I shall use some Kantian terminology. Since it is possible that my understanding of this terminology is non-standard, I should emphasize that the main point at issue here is not whether my understanding of the terminology is authentically Kantian, but whether the arguments framed using the terminology are cogent. With that in mind, here are two points about terminology. First, I shall treat the phrase 'X is worthy of moral respect' as being equivalent to 'It is impermissible to treat X merely as a means to an end'; and I shall assume that if it is impermissible to treat X merely as a means to an end (i.e., if X is worthy of moral

---

[27] This line of argument was suggested to me by Antony Duff, to whom I am indebted for discussion of a number of related issues.

respect), then X can have ends that give rise to duties in other agents, simply because they are ends that X has. I shall also talk, in a way that I take to be Kantian, of agents having some ends conditionally and other ends unconditionally; and I shall also assume, with Kant, that duties are unconditional ends.

According to the objection I am considering, a capacity for remorse entails, at the very least, a capacity to grasp that one is an agent; and that one is responsible, morally, for one's actions. This is certainly plausible in the case of an individual's remorse; and claiming that collective remorse is unlike individual remorse in this respect seems uncomfortably *ad hoc*. It also seems plausible that an agent that can see itself as being morally responsible for its actions should see itself as having duties. I suggest that an advocate of the view I am defending can, and should, accept all of these points.

The objection under consideration adds to these points the claims that an agent that can see itself as having duties should be seen by others as an agent that deserves respect. I claim that the objection fails because this claim is false. However, and as we shall see, it is false in a way which is easy to miss if we assume that the only agents we are considering are individual human agents. There are two ways in which one might argue for the claim, which I take to be false. On the first line, the reasoning would be that an agent that recognizes itself as having duties is one that must regard itself as deserving of respect; and an agent that recognizes itself as worthy of respect must be regarded as worthy of respect by others. On the second line, it would be that an agent that recognizes itself as having duties should be regarded as having duties by others; and that an agent that is regarded as having duties by others should be regarded as being worthy of moral respect from others. While both of these lines of argument seem promising, I think that neither of them establishes the desired conclusion.

Consider the first. It is plausible that an individual who sees him- or herself as having duties does, for that very reason, has to see him or herself as having ends that are – in Kantian language – unconditionally valid; or, in less Kantian language, as worthy of pursuit independently of any of the agent's desires. And one might think that ends that are worthy of pursuit by an agent independently of that agent's desires give rise to reasons which ought to have weight for *any* agent. And to have ends which give rise to reasons which have weight for all agents is, one might think, to be deserving of respect. So there is something to the idea that an agent that sees itself as having duties must see itself as deserving of respect.

Does it follow that other agents should see such an agent as deserving of respect? If we restrict our attention to the case of individual agents, it might seem so. For one might think that we should, after all, see all other human beings as deserving of respect. But to say this is not to say that we should see other human beings as worthy of respect *because* they see themselves as being worthy of respect. And there is, even, a good reason not to make this latter claim; namely, that it seems to hold out the possibility of giving a moral explanation for something for which there is no (further) moral explanation and where the demand for a moral explanation is inappropriate. Arguably, the fact that we should respect other individual moral agents is a brute moral fact; not a fact that needs to be explained by reference to other facts; and *a fortiori* not by the fact that they see themselves as being worthy of respect.

This point suggests that there is little reason to think that we can argue successfully that corporations should be seen as ends-in-themselves along the lines being considered here. In order to have such an argument, we would need to think that a claim that we have to respect agents that respect themselves could ground justify a claim that we need to respect particular moral agents. I have argued that a claim of the first sort cannot explain a claim of the second sort. I now suggest that if a claim of the first sort cannot explain a claim of the second sort, then it cannot justify a claim of the second sort either. Any reason for doubting a claim of the second sort would be a reason, and indeed just as good a reason, for doubting a claim of the first sort.

So while the first argument does not look absurd, it seems likely to be unsuccessful. What about the second? We need not give much attention to the claim that a being that can see itself as having duties should be seen by others as having duties. For, the question of whether corporations should be seen as having moral duties is presumably not likely to be in dispute here. So everything depends on whether an agent that is seen as having duties should, for that reason, be seen as being worthy of respect. Here, I think that the answer is no; and that the reason why depends on the kinds of duties that corporations have.

If corporations have duties, they have ends that are unconditional. One might think that such unconditional ends would be binding on all moral agents, and that consequently their existence imposed duties on all moral agents. Suppose this is right. One might think that this meant that corporations were deserving of respect, because for a being to have ends which impose duties on all moral agents simply is for that being to deserve respect. But this is not correct. For a being to deserve respect is for it to have ends which impose moral duties on other agents *simply because they are the ends of that agent.* And corporations have no such ends. The unconditional ends that they have – and the duties that they thereby impose on other agents – involve duties that would fall on other agents in any case. So these ends do not impose moral duties on agents *simply because they are ends of the corporate agent.* If this is right, the second line of argument does not establish that corporations are deserving of moral respect. In other words it does not establish that it is impermissible to treat corporations as means to ends.

9   Does treating a collective as a means entail treating individuals as means?

In Section 8 I argued that the fact that there are collective analogies of emotions such as regret and remorse is not enough to establish that we have a duty not to treat collective entities as mere means. However, someone might argue that there is another basis on which we might argue that we have a duty not to treat collective agents as mere means – namely that if we do so, we will necessarily treat individuals as mere means. I shall now argue that it does not.

The idea that treating a collective agent as a means involves treating the individuals who make it up as means is based on two straightforward thoughts. The first is, of course, that collectives are made up of individuals. The second is that there is no way of inflicting suffering on collectives without imposing suffering on those individuals. The idea that treating a collective as a mere means involves treating its members as a means cannot simply follow from the fact that that the collective is made up of individuals. If you treat me as a mere means to an end – for example, by spreading malicious gossip about me simply for your own amusement – you do not thereby treat my arms, legs and torso as means to an end (unless, perhaps, the malicious gossip focuses on some aspect of my physical appearance).

One might say that this is simply because my arms, legs and torso are not themselves agents. This point is significant, but not decisive. It is significant, because in order for you to treat me as a mere means in a way that is morally objectionable, I must be the right kind of agent (and *a fortiori* I must be some kind of agent). But it is not decisive. In order to treat me as a mere means you must stand in the right sort of relationship – or perhaps we should say the wrong sort of relationship – to my agency. And, I shall claim, you do not stand in that sort of relationship to my agency, just because you stand in that sort of relation to the agency of some collective of which I am a part.

As we have seen, Duff holds that the prohibition on treating agents merely as means is to be interpreted as a requirement that we see them as individuals who are responsible for their own behavior. It is not clear to me that on this account of what it is to treat someone as a means, denunciatory punishments of agents need involve treating those agents merely as means to an end. Nor – as I have already observed – is it clear that there is anything wrong with treating collective bodies as means to an end. Finally, it does not seem to be true that in treating collective bodies merely as means we would thereby be treating individual members of a collective merely as means. For under certain circumstances we might think it appropriate not to treat a collective body as an agent which is responsible for its own actions, simply because those actions depended entirely on the actions of one particular individual (whom we might then hold responsible instead).

More importantly for present purposes, there is no obvious reason for thinking that if we inflict harsh treatment on a corporation, and this treatment has harmful effects those who are associated with it, we necessarily fail to treat those individuals as persons or responsible agents. Consider a situation where a large fine is imposed on a corporation. It is true that the imposition of the fine may result in harm to various individuals. Profits may be hit, harming shareholders; prices may go up, harming consumers; as market position is lost, workforces may be reduced, harming employees; managerial salaries may be reduced; and so on. However, there are two points to make about this. First, even in relatively straightforward cases in which individuals are punished for individual crimes (perhaps along lines which the communicative theorist would be willing to sanction), inflicting harsh treatment on those individuals may result in harms to other individuals who have not committed the crime in question, such as family members. Although this might, in some cases, be regarded as a reason for mitigating an individual's sentence, we would not normally regard a failure to wholly remit the sentence imposed as involving the treatment of the criminal's family members as means to an end.

Secondly, in the corporate case, and particularly in cases where fines are imposed on corporations, there is a further reason for denying that any resulting harms involve the punishing authority's treating affected individuals as means to an end. For, in case like this, the identities of the individuals affected and the exact nature of the harms that result will normally depend to a large extent on decisions made at the corporate level. This means we have reasons for not regarding the harms which are inflicted as ways in which the *punishing authority* treats shareholders, consumers, workers or managers. To see things in that manner would be to deny the agency of the corporate decision makers. *A fortiori*, they should not be seen as ways in which the punishing authority treats individuals as means to an end.[28]

Now consider O'Neill's account of what it is for an agent to treat another agent as a means. It is worth noticing, as a preliminary matter, that on this account it is far from obvious how many of the forms of punishment that an advocate of a denunciatory view of punishment might wish to see imposed on corporate bodies would actually involve treating those bodies as means to an end. For example, it is not obvious that a corporation could not consent to a maxim according to which corporations that were found to have breached certain kinds of regulatory standards should be subjected to large fines. In fact, corporations might have good reasons for consenting to such maxims. For, if generally followed, such maxims might reduce the extent to which corporations with law-abiding decision-makers were not put in an unfavorable position vis-à-vis their competitors. (Furthermore, it seems plausible that if corporate bodies can consent to being treated in such ways, so can the individuals who make them up.)

Nevertheless, one might argue that if one understands the prohibition on treating agents as means to an end in the way that O'Neill suggests, some forms of punishment of which the denunciatory theorist might approve could involve treating collective bodies as means to an end. Consider, for example, what is sometimes known as the 'corporate death penalty', where in response to particularly heinous forms of corporate wrongdoing a corporation is actually dissolved.[29] It might turn out that for certain formal reasons a corporation could not consent to its own dissolution.[30] There might also be formal reasons why a corporation might not be able to consent to measures which would reduce its profitability: for example, it might be constituted in such a way as to require

---

[28] There might be some forms of punishment of collective bodies to which this argument could not be applied. One example might be punishing a nation by instituting a boycott which affects all citizens falling into a particular category. What makes the difference in those kinds of cases seems to be that the collective body has little or no way of influencing the way in which the punishment impacts on its members. For further discussion, see Pasternak 2011.

[29] Fisse and Braithwaite 1993 pp. 143–4.

[30] I have in mind, for example, a situation where, say, a certain set of constitutional arrangements is written into something analogous to French's corporate decision structure, and these arrangements rule out the possibility of the corporation consenting to its own dissolution.

it, as a matter of policy, to pursue policies that would maximize share-holder value. If it was true that, on O'Neill's account of treating an agent as a mere means, in treating a collective as a mere means to an end one was thereby treating some or all of the members of the collective as mere means to an end, then it might follow that punishments of corporate bodies of this sort would involve treating individuals as mere means to ends.

However, on O'Neill's account, it is not true that in treating a collective as a mere means one thereby treats the individuals that make it up as mere means. This is because it simply does not follow from the fact that a collective could not consent to the maxim of some agent's action that none of the individuals who make up the collective could consent to this. In fact, it is not clear to me that there is any reason why they could not all consent to it. This is because, on a plausible account of collective consent, a collective can consent to something without all its members consenting to it; and all the members of the collective can consent to something without the collective consenting to it.

Consider, for example, an account of collective consent modeled on Gilbert's work.[31] Collective consent would involve a form of joint commitment on the part of some individuals, to consent as a body to certain treatment. The individuals might do so while being individually convinced that the treatment was inappropriate. Or, more relevantly for the current discussion, they might each individually be convinced that the treatment was appropriate, while being unable to express a collective commitment to that view. (They might, for example, each take themselves to be morally required – for example by means of a previously given promise – to act in ways which served the interests of the other individual members of the collective body.) This means that it would be possible – at least in principle – for a collective to be treated in ways to which it was unable to consent without this entailing that the individuals in question were unable to be treated in this way. In other words, it is possible for a collective to be treated as a mere means without any individual being treated as a mere means.

This argument establishes the possibility in principle of a collective body being treated as a mere means without any particular individual being treated as a mere means. But one might wonder about the implications of this claim for the forms of punishment of collective bodies, which I have suggested might involve treating those bodies as means to an end. Consider, once again, the possibility of a corporate body which

---

[31] Gilbert 1989.

is, for formal reasons, unable to consent to its own dissolution (perhaps because such a possibility is ruled out by its articles of association). It would not follow from this fact about the corporation that anyone involved in the corporation should be incapable of consenting to its being wound up.

One might think that in the normal course of things those who stood to profit from the corporation's activities or those who were in leadership roles might be unwilling to consent; but this is not the point at issue, and is, in any case, not necessarily true: imagine a situation where, as a result of large-scale corporate wrongdoing the board of directors of a corporation resigns and is replaced – pending judicial proceedings by a caretaker board. Members of such a board might well be in a position to consent to the corporation in question being wound up.

10   Conclusion

I have argued that the denunciatory version of the expressive theory of punishment which I defended in Part I of this book can provide a convincing account of the practice of punishing corporations. In other words I have argued that, on the account of punishment I have offered, the punishment of corporate entities is an intelligible practice. I have not sought to address the questions about the appropriate balance to be struck between assigning criminal responsibility to collective bodies as such and assigning it to individuals acting on behalf of those corporations, or about the kinds of behavior on the part of corporate bodies we should regard as criminal offenses. These are important questions, but ones which do not fall fully within the scope of the philosophy of punishment: they are questions to be settled within a political community, and by the means similar to those that the political community employs for deciding such questions in individual cases.

8
Punishing States

1 Introduction

In Chapter 7, I considered the question of whether expressive theories of punishment, and in particular denunciatory ones, could accommodate the practice of punishing collective entities under domestic law. I argued that this practice could be best understood within the context of a denunciatory version of the expressive view that I defended in the first half of the book. In this chapter, I aim to apply some of the insights from that discussion to a rather different issue: the question of whether we should regard states as potential subjects of punishment under international criminal law.

There is an obvious and significant distinction between the task of these two chapters. As I noted at the start of Chapter 7, applying the expressive account to the punishment of collective entities under domestic law involves trying to show how we can make sense of an existing practice involving non-paradigmatic instances of legal punishment within the context of a theory developed, in the first instance, to cover paradigmatic instances of legal punishment (that is to say, those in which a political community imposes harsh treatment on an individual offender who is a member of that community). A discussion of whether states should be regarded as potential subjects of criminal punishment is rather different. For despite its name, international criminal law makes almost no provision for the idea that states – or other collective entities – can be seen as *loci* of criminal responsibility, and potential subjects of punishment. So in this case we are not concerned with trying to make sense of a practice which already exists within the context of our theory; instead, we are concerned with the question of the ways in which that practice might be revised and reformed.

Within this context, the expressive theory of punishment that I have developed is interesting for the light it sheds on two questions. The first is whether there are any conceptual barriers to regarding states as potential subjects of punishment. As far as the first issue is concerned, we might expect to have to consider two questions. The first is whether the fact that states are collective entities rules out the possibility of punishing them. In the light of the discussion of punishing collective entities in Chapter 7, it will be unsurprising that my answer to this question is 'No'. A second question which also needs to be addressed here is whether the fact that punishment involves a denunciatory judgment made by a political community about its members rules out the possibility of punishing states. Here we need to consider the question of whether states can be regarded as members of a political community in the same way that individuals can; and whether this rules out the possibility of punishing states.

Those who think our existing practices should be revised in such a way as to accommodate the possibility of punishing states face another significant obstacle. They do not simply need to show that it makes sense to think of states being punished. They also need to consider whether, and under what circumstances, it might be morally permissible to punish states. This issue arises, I shall argue, insofar as the punishment of states, like the punishment of collective entities under domestic law seems likely to involve treating them harshly, and treating states harshly seems likely to entail inflicting suffering on the members of those states. Consequently it is unclear whether there are any ways in which states may permissibly be punished.

I shall argue that this consideration does not rule out the possibility of punishing states, but does place significant constraints on the ways in which we can permissibly do so. I consider three kinds of punitive measure which we might consider taking against states: punitive war;[1] economic measures, such as sanctions; and what I call 'status measures' – which involve suspending some of the rights and privileges typically associated with statehood (,such as rights of membership in international organizations, rights of diplomatic representation, state sovereignty privilege and so on). I shall argue that although all three kinds of measure run the risk of inflicting harm on citizens of a state, only the first two are ruled out as potentially permissible forms of punishment.

In making this case I shall draw on two important conceptual resources. One is, of course the version of the expressive theory of punishment I

---

[1] Luban 2012.

defended in the first part of the book. The second is a taxonomy, first proposed by Toni Erskine, which allows us to distinguish between different kinds of ways in which the punishment of states might harm citizens. Erskine's analysis concentrates exclusively on the case of punitive war. However, it also raises questions about other kinds of punitive measures – in particular, the Status Measures and Economic Measures on which my analysis focuses.

Erskine's taxonomy distinguishes between 'Guilt By Association', 'Misdirected Harms', and 'Overspill'. In 'Guilt by Association' we treat individuals as being guilty of actions for which their states are (supposedly) being punished; in 'Misdirected Harm' we deliberately inflict forms of undeserved harm on individuals as if this harm was deserved; and in 'Overspill' we causing indirectly or adventitious harms to individuals without deliberately targeting them for harm. Erskine suggests that these different kinds of harms are problematic in different ways and to different extents. In particular she holds that Overspill Harms do not provide us with a reason for finding the punishment of states problematic, since we typically regard them as irrelevant in the domestic case; that Guilt By Association is relatively easy to avoid, and that the problem of Misdirected Harm places the greatest obstacles in the way of punishing states.

Although I take Erskine to be correct about the significance of the distinction between Misdirected Harms and Overspill Harms, I shall argue that Guilt By Association is harder to avoid than Erskine supposes. One advantage of the denunciatory theory of punishment which I have developed in this book, and which I shall be applying to the case of states, is precisely that it does provide us with a way of distinguishing between ways of punishing states which do, and ways which do not, involve morally problematic forms of Guilt By Association.

2   Are states punishable?

I noted earlier that International Criminal Law makes currently makes little provision for regarding states (or other collective entities) as things which can be punished. There are obvious practical considerations which explain why this should be so. Nevertheless, as Antony Lang has noted, a close examination of the historical record suggests that the possibility of regarding states, as well as individuals, as liable for crimes has at times received non-negligible diplomatic support.[2]

---

[2] Lang 2007.

It is worth considering what kinds of consideration might constitute a *prima facie* case for this view. In doing so I shall take for granted that we can make sense of the idea of a collective agent, whose actions can be considered as distinct from – though in many cases depending on – the actions of the individuals who make up those collectives;[3] that states, in particular, are often properly viewed as collective agents;[4] and that on at least some accounts of punishment it makes sense to see collective agents as potential subjects of punishment.[5] While controversial in some contexts, these nevertheless represent mainstream philosophical positions.

Mark Drumbl has suggested there may be good pragmatic reasons for regarding collectives, and not just individuals, as being among the entities which can be punished for crimes against humanity.[6] He notes that a focus on individual perpetrators within domestic legal systems can overwhelm those systems, and suggests that prosecuting individuals in international tribunals also risks undermining some of the purposes which we might hope that trials for atrocities might serve. For example the long delays which form a natural part of such trials seem to undermine the possibility that they might play a role in processes of reconciliation. (This is especially so, perhaps, in respect of the expressive functions which we might hope the practice of responding to atrocities under form of law might embody.)[7]

However this leaves open the question of whether states, considered as one particular kind of collective agent, should be seen as potential subjects of punishment. A consideration of the subject matter of international criminal law – and especially the 'Nuremberg trio' of war crimes, crimes against humanity, and crimes against peace, and the slightly more recently recognized crime of genocide – suggests they could be. Many of these crimes have an obvious collective dimension in which states, as collective agents, are implicated.

Consider the crime of waging aggressive war.[8] Since wars can only be fought by states, or by groups which resemble states in certain

---

[3] French 1984; List and Pettit 2011; Hess 2014.

[4] Stilz 2011; Wendt 2004; Pasternak 2013.

[5] For further defense of this view see Chapter 7 and Wells 2001.

[6] Mark Drumbl 2007, 2011. See also Luban 2007.

[7] Drumbl raises other issues too, including considerations of equity – he raises the possibility that there might be something wrong with a situation where the due process rights of individuals accused of atrocities in international tribunals are given as greater degree of protection than the rights of defendants charged with less serious crimes in domestic legal systems.

[8] May 2008.

paradigmatic respects, it seems natural of think of the waging of aggressive war as a crime committed by states. This is also true of some kinds of war crimes involving violation of *jus in bello* norms. If it is part of the military policy of a state to ignore such norms, then we have something which involves criminal action on the part of the state, and not just of the individuals who carry out that policy. (This need not rule out the possibility of similar crimes being carried out in a 'freelance' capacity by individuals who are not carrying out the policy of a state.)[9]

This does not show that a legal code which attempts to cover genocide and the Nuremberg trio must recognize collective agents – still less states considered as one particular kind of collective agent – among their perpetrators. International criminal law in its current form does not. Some might suggest that there are deep conceptual or moral reasons for this. Practitioners of law and non-practitioners who theorize about law sometimes suppose that relatively deep structural features of a form of law – such as the fact that international law does not regard states as being potential subjects of punishment – must reflect some kind of deep conceptual truth.

However, this is an illusion. The existence of any system of law – and of the system of international law – is a great practical, moral and conceptual achievement. It does not follow that every central feature of such a system must represent some kind of moral, practical or conceptual necessity. Sometimes the historical record shows that significant features of a legal system are the result of fairly contingent historical circumstances. An examination of the International Law Commission's Committee on State Responsibility suggests that this may be the case here.

The Committee on State Responsibility debated the question of whether states could be regarded as criminal between 1956 and 2002. The Draft Articles submitted to the ILC in 2001 followed the recommendations of France, Ireland, Japan, the UK and the USA in not explicitly allowing for the possibility of state criminality. However, several countries, including Denmark, Italy, Mongolia and Greece argued that there should be such a provision. Furthermore the Special Rapporteur of the committee argued for the coherence of the notion, but suggested that it should be omitted from the Draft Articles because they made no mention of the sorts of institutional mechanisms it would require.[10]

---

[9] Similarly Meckled-Garcia (2008) has argued that crimes against humanity have a distinctive nature, which means that they can only be committed by states, or by individuals acting as representatives of the state.

[10] Lang 2007.

(This suggests that he at least saw the issue as being practical rather than conceptual.) It is implausible to suggest that matters *could not* have ended up differently, and that the views of Denmark, Italy, Mongolia and Greece could not have prevailed.

Some authors suggest that if we regard states as the kinds of agents which are capable of committing crimes, individuals will be able to sidestep responsibility for the actions involved in initiating aggressive wars, participating in state-sponsored violations of *jus in bello* norms, or violating human rights. However, the choice here is not between a form of international law which treats only states as potential criminals under international law and one which treats only individuals as such. It is between one which treats only individuals as potential perpetrators of crimes and one which treats both states and individuals as potential perpetrators of distinct, but in many cases, closely related crimes. There is no obvious bar to treating both certain kinds of action committed by states, and certain kinds of actions performed by individuals in the pursuit of those crimes as criminal actions.

3 The harsh treatment and expressive conditions on punishment

I have argued that there are no conceptual obstacles in the way of thinking that states were agents capable of committing crimes under international law. Might the nature of punishment prevent us from thinking of them as the sorts of entities which are capable of undergoing punishment?

As we have already seen, punishment is typically taken to involve: (1) harsh treatment directed at an agent, by (2) an appropriate official (3) in response to a breach of a law. Furthermore it was a key claim of this book that harsh treatment can only constitute punishment if (4) it is imposed in pursuit of the right kind of expressive goals.[11] There seems little difficulty with the idea that states can satisfy conditions (2) and (3).

Matters are less obvious with condition (1): the 'harsh treatment' condition. In Chapter 7 I noted that if we understand the notion of

---

[11] In Wringe 2010 I argued that the 'appropriate official' condition is only satisfied if the harsh treatment with the right kind of expressive goals is imposed by those who are in a position to speak on behalf of a community whose laws have been violated. This point raises interesting issues that I am unable to address here for reasons of space, but does not undermine any of the claims I wish to defend here.

harsh treatment in a way that depends in a significant manner on the idea that harsh treatment causes (or is intended to cause) suffering, then it will be hard to see how it is possible to punish any kind of collective agent. I also suggested at that point that although we cannot think of collective agents as suffering, we can see them as having interests; and I suggested that we take a corporation to have been treated harshly if it is treated in a way which is damaging to its interests.[12] A similar suggestion seems appropriate in this context as well: we can take a state to have been treated harshly if it is treated in a way which is damaging to its interests.

These interests of a state are typically related in a relatively indirect way to the interests of its citizens. Often what is in the interests of a state will be in the interests of at least some of its citizens. But the reverse need not be true. Consider the case of an extremely oppressive and inefficient state. It may be that it would be in the interest of almost all the citizens of that state for it to be dissolved or annexed: perhaps the individual members of that state would find themselves better clothed and fed, more easily able to avail themselves of redress for injustice, and so on.[13]

What about the expressive considerations? In Chapter 7 I argued that in attempting to apply insights from the expressivist tradition to the punishment of corporate agents, we should focus on denunciatory rather than communicative versions of the expressive view. However, it is not immediately clear whether this line of argument is applicable to the case of punishing states. Here is one obvious difficulty with the idea. On the denunciatory conception of punishment which was defended in the first half of the book, the punishing agent was a political community whose laws had been breached. In what I called the paradigmatic case of punishment, I conceived of the state as a collective agent which was

---

[12] Antony Duff (personal communication) has suggested that we might instead argue that states can be burdened, and argue that harsh treatment is treatment which burdens a state. However, it is unclear to me that an entity can be burdened, in the sense intended, without having interests.

[13] In correspondence, Antony Duff suggested that we should regard it as being constitutive of a state that it should have regard to the interests of (presumably) all of its citizens, and that states which fail to do so should be seen not as true states, but as failed approximations to being states (just as Socrates suggests in the *Republic* that rulers who do not really aim at the interests of their citizens are not really rulers). If so, the subject matter of this chapter is not the punishment of states but the punishment of entities which purport to be states. However, none of the substantive claims I make are affected: in particular it seems hard to deny that purported states are agents or that they can have interests.

expressing the denunciatory attitudes which I took to play a central role in punishment. It is clear how this idea can be extended to cover the case of the punishment of corporations under domestic law. However, when we consider the punishment of states, we need to consider what could play the role of the agent whose attitudes are expressed in punishment.

For reasons which are analogous to those which I put forward in Chapter 3, it would probably be unhelpful to think of the punishment of states as involving the expression of attitudes of either judges involved in international tribunals, or of those who might have the responsibility of enforcing penalties which might be imposed on states under a version of international law revised in such a way as to allow for the punishment of states. A more plausible, though not entirely unproblematic, suggestion would be to see penalties inflicted under international law as expressing the attitudes of a collective body whose members were states – in other words, a collective of collectives which we might refer to as 'the international community'.

If we adopt this suggestion it is not entirely clear that the arguments that I put forward in Chapter 7 in favor of a denunciatory conception of punishment can be transferred to the case of the punishment of states in a straightforward manner. Those arguments depended on the thought that even if we think that collectives can undergo the kinds of affective states that are central to the communicative view, remorse and regret expressed by corporate agents does not have the same kind of significance as it does in the case of individual agents. We aspire to live in the kinds of political communities whose individual members can see themselves as enjoying full-fledged membership on equal terms. By contrast, it would be somewhat eccentric to value the integration of corporate agents into our domestic political community in the same way.[14]

However, it is not at all eccentric to think that if states themselves are seen as individual members of an over-arching political community, we should value the possibility of their interacting with one another on

---

[14] This is not to deny that the expression of remorse and regret by a corporate agent might not have some kind of value to its victims. See Radzik 2009 pp. 175 ff. for an interesting discussion of collective atonement. However it is not clear that this value could be realized via the imposition of punishments on collective agents. Note, in any case, that by locating the value of collective regret in the value to victims of statements of regret we have moved a long way from the idea that the agent's regret is valuable in and of itself: those who defend a communicative theory in the domestic case do not typically require that individuals who are punished make explicit statements of regret to their victims. (I thank Ambrose Lee for pressing me on this.)

equal terms in the same way that we would value this within a state of individuals. So one might think that in this context there was still a case to be made for a version of a communicative view. Nevertheless, I think there are two considerations which point away from a communicative version of expressivism and towards a denunciatory version, even in this case. The first is that we might hope to find some kind of justification of the punishment of states which might make it legitimate to punish states that do not appear to value integration into an international community on equal terms. Such states certainly appear to exist: we might think that both North Korea and the United States of America provide obvious examples of such states. (And whereas we might reasonably think that individuals who reject this goal are missing a substantive truth about what is conducive to their flourishing, it is far from obvious that something analogous applies to states that reject this view.)

Secondly, we might doubt whether there is a plausible case for thinking that collective analogues of individual regret could play a role in re-integrating states into a community of states interacting as equals. It would take substantial empirical investigation of a sort which no-one has undertaken to establish this view; and it certainly does not follow straightforwardly from the plausibility of an analogous claim in the case of the punishment of individuals (even if one takes that case to be well-established). Furthermore, there is an obvious and significant difficulty with establishing the case on empirical grounds: namely the paucity of examples of states being punished along the lines envisaged whose subsequent evolution one might hope to study.

Taken together, these two considerations suggest that, just as in the case of punishment of corporations under domestic law, it is the denunciatory version of the expressive view which is worth exploring in this context; and I shall, accordingly concentrate on it in the remainder of this chapter.[15]

4　Moral objections to punishing states: the case of punitive war

I have argued that states can be viewed as potential loci of criminal agency under international law, and that there are no conceptual obstacles to holding that states can be punished. There might nevertheless be

---

[15] I am grateful to Ambrose Lee for comments on an earlier draft of this chapter which forced me to develop the arguments of this section in more detail. (He should not be held responsible for the results.)

reasons why the punishment of states can never be morally acceptable, or reasons for placing moral constraints on the ways in which they can be punished. As David Luban notes, the punishment of states has traditionally often involved punitive war.[16] We might be wary of any view which increases the number of grounds which one state might have for going to war with another. If the only form of punishment appropriate to states was punitive war, this might be a reason for abandoning the idea that states can be punished. Nevertheless, it is worth looking in more detail at some of the reasons why punitive war seems morally problematic. For these reasons, or closely related ones, may also apply to punitive measures against states that do not involve war.

Luban considers two objections to the notion of punitive war. One is that no state can satisfy the 'appropriate authority' condition, which I mentioned briefly in Section 3. I set this issue aside. If we think that international law imposes a set of binding norms on states, we have already rejected this view of the sovereignty of states on which the objections rest: the idea that nobody has the authority to impose punishments on states.

Luban also argues that punitive war directs the use of force on the wrong targets. It would be natural to express this point by saying that punitive war punishes the wrong agents. However, we shall see that certain kinds of action directed at a state can harm the citizens of that state without subjecting them to punishment as such. So for now I shall simply talk of punitive war as involving mist-targeting the use of force. In addressing the issues that this point raises, it is helpful to rely on the taxonomy of ways in which punishments inflicted on states might involve wrongful harm developed by Erskine that I introduced in Section 1, and in particular her distinction between 'Guilt by Association', 'Misdirected Harm' and 'Overspill'. [17]

Erskine suggests that these three kinds of harm are problematic in very different ways. She notes that Overspill is a phenomenon that can arise in connexion with any form of punishment. When we have punished an individual who has committed a crime under domestic law, we run the risk of inflicting Overspill harms on any dependents he or she may have. Since we do not regard such Overspill harms as presenting a chal-

---

[16] Luban 2012.
[17] Erskine 2010. Erskine's work depends heavily on the idea that sovereign states are agents of a sort that are capable of being held morally responsible and blamed for their actions.

lenge to the legitimacy of the institution of punishment as such, we should not think it presents a special challenge to punishing states.[18]

By contrast Guilt By Association and Misdirected Harm seem problematic in ways which we would regard as undermining the legitimacy of punishment in the domestic case. Guilt By Association seems to involve a kind of category error: we are treating individuals as being responsible for actions for which – if the case that has been made for regarding states as subject to punishment is a good one – they should not be regarded as being responsible. Misdirected Harm is problematic in a different way: it breaks the link between being guilty and legitimately coming to be subject to harms that one would not otherwise be subject to.

Erskine claims that the challenge posed by Guilt By Association can be met more easily than that posed by Misdirected Harm. She argues that whereas nothing requires us to see the citizens of delinquent states as themselves being guilty of the actions their states perform, Misdirected Harm 'threatens to undermine the logic of a form or punishment.' Since states are corporate bodies with, as the well-known phrase puts it, 'no body to kick and no soul to be damned', it is hard to see how we can punish states without deliberately harming particular individuals. Since the actions of states should not be identified with those of individuals, such harms seem certain to be, in her terms, 'Misdirected'.

Expressive accounts of punishment provide some support for the idea that in the case of punitive war we can distinguish between Guilt By Association and Misdirected Harm. On a denunciatory account, acts of war will need to satisfy at least two conditions in order to constitute 'punitive war'. They will need to constitute harsh treatment and they will need to be aimed at condemning some kind of behavior on the part of that state. It seems possible, at least in principle, for warlike acts which satisfied these conditions to avoid constituting punishment of the state's citizens. For although the individuals who are targeted in acts of punitive war will be treated in a way that is harsh under a conception of harshness which is appropriate for individuals, we might take the expressive dimension of these warlike acts as being aimed at the state itself rather than at its citizens.

However the distinction Erskine wishes to make here seems less straightforward than she suggests. She illustrates the ways in which punishment directed at a state might avoid Guilt By Association by citing statements from the Iraq war of 2003, in which Tony Blair and George Bush declared that their enemy was not the people of Iraq but

---

[18] See Section 8 below for further discussion.

the regime.[19] However we cannot read the expressive dimension of acts of harsh treatment off from the statements of those who inflict that treatment as straightforwardly as Erskine's example suggests. Those dimensions also depend on how that treatment is likely to be understood by those who suffer it and those who are aware of it.[20]

Any distinction between warlike behavior directed at the citizens of a state and warlike behavior directed at the state itself would need to be reflected in some way in the behavior of the state engaging in acts of war. Some forms of warfare might allow for distinctions between what we might call the military targets and the expressive targets of military action. Consider a state whose armed forces consisted of both citizens and mercenaries. A military campaign which concentrated its attacks on army units which consisted of citizens rather than mercenaries might be regarded as one which was directing its response at the state rather than at mercenaries, particularly if it did so in situations which put the attacking force at a military disadvantage. However it seems unrealistic to suppose that any actual military campaign would pursue expressive goals in this way. In any case it is the wrong kind of distinction for our purposes: we need a distinction between state and citizens, not between citizens and non-citizens.

Could forms of military action which made a careful attempt to observe a distinction between combatants and non-combatants constitute a form of expression directed at the state rather than its citizens? The idea here would be that in selecting military personnel as the targets of action, an attacking force could be seen as directing harsh treatment at individuals in their capacity as agents of the state, while in avoiding selecting non-combatants as targets the attacking force would be refraining from treating all the inhabitants in this way.

There are two problems with this proposal. First, states already have reasons to distinguish strongly between combatants and non-combatants. This is a standard 'in bello' restriction on the use of force, embodied in international law. So a state's making this distinction in cases of punitive war would, be over-determined. Secondly, it is not clear why we should take state's action being targeted in this way as embodying the right kind of distinction. Even in times of war, military personnel are not unique in their status as agents of the state. So it is not clear why we should take violence directed at members of military forces – but not at civil servants, or the employees of state broadcasting services or

---

[19] Erskine 2010.
[20] Especially, on a denunciatory account, the latter.

hospitals – as embodying harsh treatment directed at the state itself, rather than at the military personnel of the state. (Indeed, since many military personnel are conscripts, and many of them are carrying out relatively trivial tasks, violence directed at them rather than at civilian government officials might seem a particularly inapt way of expressing condemnation of the behavior of a state.)[21] In short Erskine is wrong: punitive war is likely to involve both Misdirected Harm and Guilt By Association.[22]

5 Non-war punishments and 'Guilt by Association'

There are at least two broad classes of ways in which states could be treated that might plausibly count as forms of punishment and which fall short of war. I call these 'Economic Measures' and 'Status Measures'. Economic Measures are aimed at undermining the economic prosperity of the state and its citizens. They include such things as economic sanctions and trade boycotts. Status Measures target the standing of a state as a fully-fledged member of the international community. They might include such things as cultural boycotts and the downgrading of participatory status in international organizations, as well as measures which target the officials of a state in their capacity as representatives of that state.

Are Economic Measures or Status Measures rightly regarded as forms of punishment? Let us take it for granted that both kinds of measures could, in principle be imposed in response to some particular wrong-doing by an appropriate authority. Can they meet the Harsh Treatment and Expressive Conditions? I argued in Section 3 that measures would

---

[21] In correspondence, Antony Duff suggested that standard *in bello* constraints on attacking non-combatants depend on a view of just war as defensive war, and that different constraints might apply in the case of punitive war. If so, a refusal to attack non-combatants counts as being expressive in the right kind of way. I find this suggestion unpersuasive: although there is a recent philosophical tradition (McMahan 2009) of treating the scope of *in bello* constraints as being related to the purposes pursued in war (and thus of constraining different parties to a war in asymmetrical ways), a plausible account of the expressive dimension of a form of action should presumably consider the ways that action is likely to be understood by those on the receiving end of it, rather than by philosophers. Outside the philosophy seminar room such considerations are typically thought to constrain different parties to a conflict symmetrically.

[22] This is not supposed to exclude the possibility that it might be problematic on other grounds as well.

meet the 'Harsh Treatment' condition if they could be seen as harming the interests of the state. Status Measures seem to do so. We grant the status of a state to certain collective entities – allowing them to participate in the system of states as full members, to sign treaties, to participate in international institutions and so on – precisely because we see them as having interests which are best served by allowing them this status. Of course, we also believe that allowing states to pursue their interests in this way is on the whole, in the interests of their citizens.

Status Measures also seem capable of having the right kind of expressive function to qualify as punishment. Admittedly, they need not have this expressive function. A state's participation in certain kinds of international institutions might be suspended on purely pragmatic grounds – for example, if internal turmoil made the state's own institutions dysfunctional or if that dysfunction threatened to undermine the workings of the institution. Furthermore, there are circumstances where the imposition of Status Measures on a state might be correctly interpreted as nothing more than result of *Realpolitik* on the part of one or more powerful states.

Nevertheless under the right kind of conditions, Status Measures could have the right kind of expressive role to count as punishment. Conditions which might be relevant would include the existence of a clear set of norms, with corresponding penalties; some kind of due process norms to ensure that Status Measures were not imposed arbitrarily; and a clear statement of conditions compliance with which would be sufficient to allow the Status Measures to be rescinded.[23]

What about Economic Measures? They too will often meet the Harsh Treatment condition. We cannot identify the economic interests of the citizens of a state with the interests of a state; although many states treat the economic well-being of its citizens as a goal, not all states do so. (Consider North Korea.) However, in harming the economic interests of the citizens of a state we will often be harming the interests of the state. It is typically in the interest of a state to be able to raise money from its citizens by taxing their economic activities. The less prosperous its citizens are, the less revenue it is likely to be able to raise, and the less easily it will be able to pursue its interests.

---

[23] Space precludes offering a detailed account of how international criminal trials might work in practice. However, there seems no reason of principle why some of the sorts of judicial institutions which deal with individuals, such as the ICC, could not also deal with criminal charges against states.

Some kinds of economic measures are already regarded as having a denunciatory function in the international sphere (as they can in the domestic sphere): campaigns in the 1980s and 1990s to persuade banks and other companies to disinvest from South Africa provide an example. It is relatively easy to see why: what clearer way could there be, one might ask, to communicate one's disapproval of certain kinds of activity than by cutting one's economic ties with the agents that engage in that activity. Even if this were not true, it seems fairly easy to see how Economic Measures could be endowed with the right kind of expressive significance.

Unlike punitive war, the imposition of Status Measures seems to be a way in which we can punish states without punishing their citizens. Status Measures can, in principle, involve harsh treatment of states without involving harsh treatment of individuals. For states often operate in ways which are not in the interest of all of their citizens. Furthermore the imposition of Status Measures need be taken to involve any form of denunciation of the citizens of a state. Whether it is correctly so taken in any given case will depend on whether the actions being denounced can legitimately be seen as being the actions of the citizens of that state. I shall discuss the circumstances in which this can be so in more detail in a moment.[24] If Status Measures are imposed in ways which do not constitute harsh treatment or which do not constitute an expressive denunciation of citizens, they should also not be seen as punishing those citizens. They avoid Guilt By Association.

Economic Measures contrast with Status Measures in this respect. Economic Measures seem inevitably to require inflicting harsh treatment on the citizens of a state. So in order to avoid Guilt By Association, Economic Measures will need to be understood as expressing disapproval of a state rather than of its citizens. For otherwise they will involve harsh treatment with a denunciatory expressive role aimed at the citizens of a state – in other words, punishment. However, it is not clear how economic measures could be seen as expressing disapproval of a state rather than of the citizens whose economic prosperity they affect.

Here is one possibility. We might say that the Economic Measures express denunciation of the state because the individuals whose prosperity is being targeted are only targets insofar as they are citizens of the

---

[24] For further, more detailed discussion, see Section 7 below.

state. This view seems difficult to sustain. For one thing, it is not clear what we will say about the position of resident aliens in a state subject to Economic Measures. However it is difficult, perhaps, to imagine Economic Measures being crafted in such a way as to fall only on citizens of a state and not on others associated with it.

6 Non-war punishments: misdirected and overspill harms

In Section 5, I argued that Status Measures need not necessarily involve harsh treatment of the citizens of a state, and that we need not see their denunciatory expressive function as being directed at citizens of a state. In other words, they need not involve Guilt By Association. However, they will often involve actions which harm the interests of the citizens of a state against which they are taken. States which are deprived of a full role in international institutions will have fewer opportunities to advance the economic interests of their citizens; an inability to negotiate treaties will put their citizens at risk, and restricting the applicability of state sovereignty privileges will mean that states will face difficulties in exploiting their economic resources. We need to consider whether such harms should be classified alongside Overspill Harm, which would not undermine the legitimacy of such forms of punishment; or as Misdirected Harms, which would.

Here is an argument for considering the negative effects that Status Measures have on the citizens of a state as being Overspill Harms rather than Misdirected Harms. It is a necessary condition of a harm's counting as misdirected that the individuals who suffer from it be regarded as the targets of that harm. This need not involve them being individually picked out as targets for that harm. However, it does require us to see situations in which they are indeed harmed in certain specific ways as successes, and situations where they are not harmed in those ways as failures. Status Measures do not appear to satisfy the condition.

It is at least possible to envisage circumstances in which Status Measures benefit, rather than harm individual citizens – for example, by forcing governments to reconsider oppressive policies, or by destabilizing a regime which treats its citizens in an oppressive manner. The fact that Status Measures had an effect in this kind of situation would not necessarily be regarded as a failure of those measures. In many circumstances, they might instead be treated as a success. But if this is so, it seems as though it would be a mistake to classify harms to individual citizens caused by Status Measures as Misdirected Harms. They should instead be seen as Overspill Harms.[25] (Notice that I am not claiming that Status Measures frequently, or indeed ever, benefit citizens of a state in the way in which I have suggested. This is an empirical claim, and which seems, *prima facie,* implausible. The point is one about the conditions under which we would think that a course of action had gone awry.)

Now consider Economic Measures. I have argued that they might be crafted in such a way as to avoid Guilt By Association. However they seem inevitably to involve Misdirected Harm. For there is no way of attacking the economic interests of a state which does not involve attacking the economic interests of its citizens. Economic measures which had the result of making citizens of a state which was being punished more prosperous would, on that ground alone, be regarded as a failure. So we cannot avoid seeing the citizens whose prosperity is affected by Economic Measures as the targets of these measures.

Someone might argue that in at least some cases, the sorts of harms I am describing here should not be regarded as 'Misdirected'. One argument for doing so would involve distinguishing between legitimate and illegitimate states. The suggestion to be considered would be that in states which meet certain conditions of legitimacy, the acts of the state could legitimately be attributed to the citizens. In such cases, harms befalling citizens as a result of Economic Measures could not be regarded as Misdirected. Instead, we might argue, citizens of such states have made themselves liable for the actions of the states of which they are members. The same would not apply to states which did not meet these conditions.

We might wonder about the status of economic harms to non-citizens (or, more generally, those who are not permitted to be full participants in the political life of the community) on this proposal. Such individuals could presumably not be regarded as having made themselves liable for the acts of the state in the way that citizens had. A natural response is that although we cannot regard harms to the economic interests

---

[25] I have argued that an action cannot be seen as targeting X for harsh treatment if a failure to treat X harshly is not viewed as being *ipso facto* a failure of the action. But couldn't someone argue along the same lines that normal cases of punishment don't target offenders, since we wouldn't regard it as a failure of our punitive system if it succeeded in rehabilitating – and thus, not harming, offenders? I think the right thing to say here is that punishment does not target criminals for harm, but for harsh treatment, and that harsh treatment is treatment which would *typically* cause suffering. If we fail to inflict such treatment on an offender, we fail to punish them. But we don't fail if we fail to make them suffer, or indeed if we benefit them.

of citizens as being Overspill Harms on the grounds that Economic Measures that ended up benefitting these citizens would be regarded as having failed, the same does not appear to apply to Economic Measures which benefitted non-citizens.

7 Feasibility in a system of law

The upshot of the preceding discussion would appear to be one which allowed for a two-tier system of punishments under International Law. One kind of punishment, involving 'Status Measures', would be applicable to states of all sorts. Another, involving 'Economic Measures', would be applicable to states that met certain criteria of legitimacy, of a sort which would allow for the state's actions to be regarded as also being actions of the citizens.

For this suggestion to be useful, we would need to be able to describe in detail the criteria which states needed to meet in order to count as liable. Many of the states whose actions might turn out to be punishable under international law might fail to meet these criteria. Perhaps only a few would meet them. If so, the cases under which Economic Measures could be imposed as a form of punishment would be fairly limited. It might nevertheless be applicable to, say, the citizens of nominally democratic states involved in committing the crime of aggressive war.

This suggestion seems attractive in many respects. For example, the idea that citizens of legitimate states should be liable to more severe consequences than the citizens of illegitimate states might appear to accord with some of our intuitions about natural justice. Furthermore, we might hope that an awareness of these potential consequences might lead citizens to restrain their political leaders from pursuing courses of action forbidden under international law. However, I shall now argue that a two-tier system of this sort is unsustainable.

Throughout this I have been concerned with the sorts of ways in which states might be regarded as liable to punishment under a possible system of international law. I have been less concerned with what one might call 'extra-judicial' forms of punishment. I now wish to argue that considerations of the form that an international legal system might take should rule out the kind of two-tier system of punishments that is envisaged here.

Here is one kind of concern. Any practicable system of international law will require widespread support. This support will need to come in part – though hopefully not exclusively – from states which meet the criteria of legitimacy that, on the account proposed, would open them up to the possibility of Economic Measures. Someone might doubt that a system of law under which legitimate states were made subject to a wider range of possible punishments than illegitimate states would be likely to enjoy widespread support from legitimate states. This concern might seem weighty to many of those interested in questions of feasibility. However, I have abstracted from such considerations so far. It might seem somewhat question-begging to appeal to them at this stage.

Here is a different concern. The two-tier system involved would require international courts to make determinations as to the legitimacy or otherwise of states coming before it for judgment. We can imagine a number of ways in which such determinations might be made. For example, it might be up to individual judicial bodies to make these determinations whenever a court was dealing with allegedly criminal behavior on the part of a state. Alternatively, such determinations might be made by an independent body on a regular rather than an *ad hoc* basis.

On either kind of system, it would presumably be necessary for the relevant conditions of legitimacy to be set out under international law. However, doing so seems likely to involve two kinds of problem. First, there is a problem of perverse incentives. States which perceived themselves to be in danger of being subject to accusations of criminal behavior might have an incentive to avoid meeting the legitimacy criteria, as a way of narrowing down the range of punitive measures to which they might be subject. While this might not be a serious problem in the case of states whose satisfaction of the legitimacy criteria was fairly well-entrenched, it might well do so in the case of states whose legitimacy was closer to the borderlines.[26]

Here is a second problem. The criteria of legitimacy accepted by an international legal system will have to be ones which enjoy widespread international support. As such, they seem likely to require a great deal of compromise. Such compromises seem likely to err on the side of generosity in their attributions of legitimacy: the sorts of criteria which are likely to be adopted are likely to be ones which will include, rather

---

[26] Matters might be different if illegitimate states were also subject to other forms of coercive intervention. However, I suspect that in practice some states are, by virtue of their geo-political position, likely to avoid the possibility of such interventions, or be less subject to them than others. Furthermore, if we make the possibility of introducing a framework for punishing states dependent on the prior existence of a framework for coercive intervention in illegitimate states, we are unlikely to see either introduced in practice. I thank Antony Duff for raising this issue.

than exclude, states as legitimate. By contrast, one might think that the criteria which a state needs to meet for its actions to be correctly regarded as being the actions of its citizens may be quite demanding. As a result there may well be mismatches between the two sets of criteria: states which are accepted as legitimate by an international legal system may not meet the criteria of legitimacy envisaged by the two-tier system of punishment. If so, such a system might well be one in which impositions of Economic Measures involved considerable risks of Misdirected Harm. By contrast, a single-tier system of punishments involving only Status Measures would avoid this risk.

8 Overspill reconsidered

Earlier, I followed Erskine in accepting that those concerned with the question of whether International Law should allow for the punishment of states should ignore what she calls 'Overspill Harms' and focus on the problems cause by what she calls 'Guilt By Association' and 'Misdirected Harm.' Ignoring Overspill Harms played a significant part in my argument for the viability of Status Measures as a way of punishing states. We might think, however, that Erskine has underestimated the significance of Overspill Harms. If so, this raises a problem for which we do not yet have a solution.

Erskine's case for ignoring Overspill Harms when thinking about the acceptability of punishing states rested on an analogy with the case of domestic punishment. As we saw, she pointed out that Overspill Harms occur in the case of domestic punishment and suggests that since we do not take such harms to undermine the legitimacy of domestic punishment, we should not take it to undermine the legitimacy of punishing states.[27] While this observation is significant, it is not the end of the story. Much depends on why exactly we think we are entitled to ignore Overspill Harms in the domestic case. To answer this question we need to consider exactly why someone might take Overspill Harms to present a problem for any form of punishment. There seem to be at least three possibilities, each of which needs to be treated slightly differently.

One reason for being concerned with Overspill Harms is that one might take punitive acts which result in harms to individuals who have committed no offense to involve punishment of the innocent. Here we need to consider two possibilities. One possibility is that the harms involved here do involve something which can correctly be described

---

[27] Erskine 2012.

as a form of punishment. In this case, we do not have an instance of Overspill, but of what Erskine calls Guilt By Association. Such cases have already been covered in our earlier discussion. A second possibility is that such harms do not constitute punishment properly so-called. Such harms may, for all that has been said so far, be wrongful. However, they do not constitute cases of wrongful punishment. We need some further account of why they are wrong.

One natural response is that although Overspill Harms may not constitute cases of wrongful *punishment,* they may nonetheless involve instances of potentially wrongful harming. Again, we might distinguish two cases here. Such cases might involve wrongful harm insofar as the individuals harmed have a right not to be harmed. Alternatively, that might involve potentially wrongful harm that is wrong on something akin to consequentialist grounds.

Someone who holds that we are entitled to ignore Overspill Harms in the domestic case will respond to these kinds of concerns in slightly different ways. In response to the suggestion that Overspill harms involve a possible violation of rights, it seems appropriate to appeal to considerations of Double Effect. In response to the suggestion that they involve harms that may be wrong on consequentialist grounds, further consequentialist considerations seem appropriate. It is not immediately obvious that both kinds of argument can be carried over without further ado to the international case.

Let us start with consequentialist considerations. In the domestic case, we would presumably argue along the following lines. Although it is true that in punishing an individual we cause indirect harms to his or her dependents, the existence of these harms is outweighed by the goods which are provided by the existence of a stable set of laws with reasonably predictable punishments. The plausibility of an argument of this sort depends on two things: the relatively narrow reach of Overspill Harms in the domestic case and the claimed benefits of a system on domestic law. It is possible to doubt whether, in general, these considerations carry over smoothly to the international case. If we are considering whether war is a legitimate form of punishment, we would have to contrast the relatively narrow reach of Overspill Harms in the domestic case with their much wider range in the international case; and whether they were outweighed by the benefits of a lawful international regime. It is far from obvious that we would reach the same conclusions as in the domestic case.

Fortunately, we have already argued against the acceptability of punitive war on other grounds. We need only consider whether Status

Measures and Economic Measures raise the same kinds of difficulty. In the case of Status Measures matters seem relatively straightforward. Such measures will typically not inflict serious harms on large groups of people. Matters are more complicated with Economic Measures, even in the limited cases where I suggested that they might be viable forms of punishment. It is certainly possible that Economic Measures taken against one state might have knock-on effects on the economies of other nearby states, and it may not be obvious that the benefits to be gained by a settled regime of international law would always outweigh them. If so, this would be a further consideration against the use of such measures as a form of punishment in international law.

So much for a consequentialist view of Overspill Harms. What should we say about the possibility that such harms violate a right not to be harmed? It seems plausible that in the domestic case, two kinds of consideration are relevant. We may also wish to say that to the extent that such harms result from knock-on effects of punishment, rather than being directly inflicted on individuals other than the offender, they involve either no violations of rights or only permissible violations of rights. A second kind of consideration relates to the nature of the harms being brought about in such cases. Some of the sorts of Overspill Harm that Erskine considers seem to be harms whose being inflicted does not violate anyone's rights. We might regard the emotional effects of an offender's being punished on a (fully able, mentally healthy) partner as falling into this category. Other kinds of harm might require restitution: consider, say, the harms that might be inflicted on a young child when a care-giver is given a custodial sentence.

Again, it is unclear whether the sorts of reasons we can give for discounting Overspill Harms in the domestic case carry over smoothly to the international case; and again they seem to apply differently in the case of Status Measures and Economic Measures. There are many different cases to consider: I shall only consider one. Take the case of a young child resident in a state which is being punished. Such a child might not be the direct target of any harms resulting from Status Measures or Economic Measures. If so, the only harms which need to be considered are Overspill harms. Assume this is in fact the case. A representative Overspill Harm resulting from a Status Measure might be the loss of opportunity to represent one's country in some international event. This seems like the kind of harm that might be discounted in the same kind of way as the harms done to a partner in the domestic case: they do not seem to involve any kinds of violations of rights. In fact, it is difficult to think of examples where Status Measures would lead to Overspill

Harms that were sufficiently serious to give rise to rights violations (or at least, to rights violations that could not be easily remedied).[28]

Matters are different when we consider Economic Measures. It seems possible that by inflicting severe damage on the economy of a country, such measures might inflict serious Overspill Harms on children resident in a country. For example, they might seriously impede the ability of parents to feed, clothe and educate their children. I suggested that in the domestic case, we might think of punishing authorities as acquiring an obligation to mitigate, remedy, or compensate such harms. It is difficult to see how authorities imposing punishments involving legal measures in the domestic realm would have the ability to discharge such obligations. This suggests that consideration about Overspill Harms might lead to the conclusion that punishments involving such measures were impermissible.

9   Conclusions

I have argued that there are no conceptual barriers in the way of seeing states as being the kinds of entities which might be subject to punishment under international law. However, I have also argued that there are significant limitations on the kinds of punishment that might legitimately be imposed upon them. The idea that punitive war should not be permitted will perhaps be uncontroversial. However, the same cannot be said of the suggestion that Status Measures are more likely to constitute legitimate forms of punishment than Economic Measures, and should be preferred to them for that reason.

This conclusion might be regarded as problematic. One reason why Economic Measures might seem preferable to Status Measures as a form of punishment is that the latter could well be seen as little more than a 'slap on the wrist'. This might seem objectionable for one of two reasons. First, punishments which are a mere 'slap on the wrist' might be seen as having little power to deter bad behavior. Secondly, such punishments might be thought to violate intuitive constraints about proportionality in punishment. Many of the criminal acts that we might regard as calling for the punishment of states are serious ones. We should expect the punishments they receive to reflect this.

---

[28] One possible and significant exception might be the loss of right to cross international borders, which might be a result of a state's right to issue passports or similar documents being withdrawn. I would argue that this kind of harm is one for which it should not be impossible to provide appropriate remedies.

These are significant objections. However, I believe that they can all be answered. One important point is that I have argued that punishments involving Economic Measures seem likely to require us to cause harms which we cannot permissibly inflict. The fact that such measures may have a significant and desirable deterrent effect does not change this fact. The same argument seems to apply to considerations of proportionality: such considerations do not outweigh our obligation not to inflict Overspill Harms.

However, there is another point which may be easy to overlook. I have argued that in some cases we should regard states as being liable to punishment under international law. However, I have not argued for a stronger conclusion, which I take to be false, namely that *only* states should be regarded as being liable to punishment under international law. Considerations about deterrence and proportionality seem likely to take on a different aspect when regarded in the context of a form of international law which allows for the punishment of both individuals and states. But that is work for another book.[29]

---

[29] In writing this chapter I have benefitted from written comments from Antony Duff, Ambrose Lee, Andrei Poama and Helen Brown Coverdale.

Bibliography

Adler, M. (2000) 'Expressive Theories of Law: A Skeptical Overview' *University of Pennsylvania Law Review* pp. 1363–1501.

Anderson, E. (1993) *Value in Ethics and Economics*. Cambridge, MA: Harvard University Press.

Ashworth A. (1988) 'Criminal Attempts and the Role of Resulting Harm under the Code and in the Common Law' *Rutgers Law Journal* 19 pp. 725–772.

Baker, A. and Erlanger, S. (2011) 'IMF chief, apprehended at airport, is accused of sexual attack.' *New York Times* May 14, 2011 http://www.nytimes.com/2011/05/15/nyregion/imf-head-is-arrested-and-accused-of-sexual-attack.html?_r=0. Accessed 24 February 2014.

Baldwin, T. (1999) 'Punishment, Communication and Resentment' in *Punishment and Political Theory.*Edited by Matravers, M. Oxford, UK: Hart Publishing..

Bass, G. (2002) *Stay the Hand of Vengeance: The Politics of War Crimes Trials*. Princeton, NJ: Princeton University Press.

Bennett, C. (forthcoming) 'Expressive Acts' in *Emotional Expression*. Edited by Smith J. and Abell C. Cambridge, UK: Cambridge University Press.

Bennett, C. (2008) *The Apology Ritual*. Cambridge, UK: Cambridge University Press.

Bennett, C. (2006) 'Taking the Sincerity Out of Saying Sorry' *Journal of Applied Philosophy* 23 pp. 147–63.

Boonin, D. (2008) *The Problem of Punishment*. Cambridge, UK: Cambridge University Press.

Braithwaite, J. (2000) 'Repentance Rituals and Restorative Justice' *Journal of Political Philosophy* 8 pp. 115–31.

Bratman, M. (2014) *Shared Agency: A Planning Theory of Acting Together*. Oxford, UK: Oxford University Press.

Bratman, M. (1992) 'Shared Cooperative Activity'. *Philosophical Review* 101(2): pp. 327–341.

Brooks, T. (2012) *Punishment*. London: Routledge.

Brooks, T. (2008) 'Shame on You, Shame on Me? Nussbaum on Shame Punishment' *Journal of Applied Philosophy* 25 pp. 322–334.

Burnyeat, Myles. (1980) 'Aristotle on Learning to Be Good'. In *Essays on Aristotle's Ethics*. Berkeley, CA: University of California Press.

Copp, D. (2006) 'On the Agency of Certain Collective Entities: An Argument from "Normative Autonomy"' *Midwest Studies in Philosophy* pp. 194–221.

Copp, D. (2010) 'Corrective Justice as a Duty of the Political Community: David Lyons on the Moral Legacy of Slavery and Jim Crow' *Boston University Law Review* 90 pp. 1731–54.

Cholbi, M. (2010) 'Compulsory Victim Restitution is Punishment' *Public Reason* 2 pp. 85–93.

Cottingham, J. (1979) 'The Varieties of Retributivism' *Philosophical Quarterly* 29 pp. 238–46.

Davidson, D. (1980) *Essays on Actions and Events*.Oxford, UK: Oxford University Press,

Davies, L. (2011) 'How Dominique Strauss-Kahn's Arrest Awoke a Dormant Anger in the Heart of France's Women.' *The Guardian* May 22, 2011 retrieved from: http://www.theguardian.com/world/2011/may/22/dominique-strauss-kahn-arrest-dormant-anger-france-women. Accessed 22 February 2014.

Drumbl, M. (2007) *Atrocity, Punishment and International Law*. Cambridge, UK: Cambridge University Press.

Drumbl, M. (2011) 'Collective Responsibility and Post-Conflict Justice' in *Accountability for Collective Wrongdoing*. Edited by Tracy Isaacs and Richard Vernon Cambridge, UK: Cambridge University Press.

Duff, R.A. (2009) 'Can We Punish the Perpetrators of Mass Atrocities' in *The Religious in Response to Mass Atrocities*. Edited by Brudholm, T. and Cushman, T. Cambridge, UK: Cambridge University Press.

Duff, R.A. (2007) *Answering for Crime: Responsibility and Liability in the Criminal Law*. Oxford, UK: Hart Publishing.

Duff, R.A. (2001) *Punishment, Communication and Community*. Cambridge, UK: Cambridge University Press.

Duff, Anthony. (1996) *Criminal Attempts*. Oxford, UK: Clarendon Press.

Duff, R.A. (1992) 'Alternatives to Punishment – or Alternative Punishments' in *Retributivism and Its Critics*. Edited by Cragg, W. Ftuttgart: Franz Steiner.

Duff, R.A. (1986) *Trials and Punishments*. Cambridge, UK: Cambridge University Press.

Duff, R.A., Farmer, L. Marshall, S. and Tadros, V. (2007) *The Trial on Trial volume 3: Towards a Normative Theory of the Criminal Trial*. Oxford, UK: Hart Publishing.

Durkheim, E. (1933) *The Division of Labour In Society*. New York: Free Press.

Dyer, C. (1999) 'Lord Denning, Controversial "People's Judge", Dies Aged 100.' *The Guardian* March 6, 1999 http://www.theguardian.com/uk/1999/mar/06/claredyer1. Accessed 12 February 2014.

Ellis, A. (2012) *The Philosophy of Punishment*. London, UK: Imprint Academic.

Ellis, A. (2003) 'A Deterrence Theory of Punishment' *Philosophical Quarterly* 53(212): 337–351.

Ellis, Anthony. (2001) 'What Should We Do With War Criminals' in *War Crimes and Collective Responsibility: A Reader*. Edited by Aleksandr Jokic pp. 97–113. Malden, MA: Imprint Academic.

Epictetus, (1928) *Discourses* 2 vols tran. W.A. Oldfather. Cambridge, MA: Harvard University Press.

Erskine, T. (2010) 'Kicking Bodies and Damning Souls: The Danger of Harming "Innocent" Individuals While Punishing "Delinquent" States'. *Ethics and International Affairs* 24 pp. 261–285.

Erskine, T. (2001) 'Assigning Responsibilities to Institutional Moral Agents: The Case of States and Quasi-States' *Ethics and International Affairs* 15 pp. 67–85.

Falls, M.M (1987) 'Retribution, Reciprocity, and Respect for Persons' In *Law and Philosophy* 6 pp. 25– 51.

Feinberg, J. (1965) 'The Expressive Function of Punishment' *The Monist* 49 pp. 397–423 reprinted in *Doing and Deserving*. Princeton, NJ: Princeton University Press.

Fisse, O. and Braithwaite, J. (1993) *Corporations, Crime and Accountability*. New York: Cambridge University Press.

Foucault, M. (1977) *Discipline and Punish: the Birth of the Prison* tr. A. Sheridan. London: Allen Lane.

French, P. (1996) 'Integrity, Intentions and Corporations' *American Business Law Journal* 34 pp. 141–156.

French, P. (1986) 'Fishing the Red Herrings Out of the Sea of Moral Responsibility' in *Actions and Events*. Edited by LePore, E. and McLaughlin, B. pp.73–87. Oxford, UK: Blackwell.

French, P. (1984) *Collective and Corporate Responsibility.* New York: Columbia University Press.

Garland, D. (1992) *Punishment and Modern Society.* Oxford, UK: Oxford University Press.

Gilbert, M. (2006) *A Theory of Political Obligation: Membership, Commitment, and the Bonds of Society.* Oxford, UK: Oxford University Press.

Gilbert, M. (2001) 'Collective Remorse' in *War Crimes and Collective Wrongdoing: A Reader.* Edited by. Jokic, A. Malden MA: Blackwell.

Gilbert, M. (1989). *On Social Facts.* London: Routledge.

Glasgow, (forthcoming) 'The Expressive Theory of Punishment Defended' *Law and Philosophy.*

Golash, D. (2005) *The Case Against Punishment: Retribution, Crime Prevention, and the Law.* New York: NYU Press.

Grice, H.P. (1989) *Studies in the Way of Words.* Cambridge, MA: Harvard University Press.

Griffiths, P. (1997) *What Emotions Really Are.* Chicago, IL: University of Chicago Press.

Gusfield, J. (1962) *Symbolic Crusade.* Urbana, IL: University of Illinois Press.

Hampton, J. (1988) 'The Retributive Idea' in *Forgiveness and Mercy.* Edited by Murphy, J. and Hampton, J. Cambridge, UK: Cambridge University Press.

Hampton, J. (1992) 'Correcting Harms Versus Righting Wrongs: The Goal of Retribution' *UCLA Law Review* 39 pp. 1659–1702.

Hanna, N. (2008) 'Say What? A Critique of Expressive Retributivism' *Law and Philosophy* 27 pp. 123–150.

Hanna, N. (2009a) 'Liberalism and the General Justifiability of Punishment' *Philosophical Studies* 145 pp. 325–349.

Hanna, N. (2009b) 'The Passions of Punishment' *Pacific Philosophical Quarterly* 90 pp. 232–250.

Hanna, N. (2014) 'Facing the Consequences' *Criminal Law and Philosophy* 8(3): pp. 589–604.

Harman, G. (1999) 'Moral Philosophy meets Social Psychology: Virtue Ethics and the Fundamental Attribution Error' *Proceedings of the Aristotelian Society* 99 pp. 315–331.

Hart, H. (1959) 'Prolegomena to the Principles of Punishment' *Proceedings of the Aristotelian Society* 60 pp. 1–26

Hart, H. (1983) 'Kelsen's Doctrine of the Unity of Law' in *says in Jurisprudence and Philosophy.* Edited by H.L.A. Hart pp. 309–42.

Hegel, G. (1942) *The Philosophy of Right* tran. T. Knox. Oxford, UK: Oxford University Press.

Hess, K. (2014) 'The Free Will of Corporations (and Other Collectives). *Philosophical Studies* 168(1): pp. 241–260.

Jeandidier, W (1991) *Droit pénal des affaires.* Paris: Dalloz.

Kelsen, Hans. (1947) 'Will the Judgment in the Nuremberg Trials Constitute a Precedent in International Law' *International Law Quarterly* 1(2).

Kelsen (1952) *Principles of International Law* New York: Rinehart

Kleinig, J. (1991) 'Punishment and Moral Seriousness' *Israel Law Review* 25 pp. 401–21.

Konstan, D. (2012) *Before Forgiveness*. Oxford, UK: Oxford University Press.

Korsgaard, C. (1996) *Creating the Kingdom of Ends*. Cambridge, UK: Cambridge University Press.

Kutz, C. (2000). 'Acting Together'. *Philosophy and Phenomenological Research* 61 pp. 1–31.

Lang, A. (2007) 'Crime and Punishment: Holding States Accountable. *Ethics and International Affairs* 21 pp. 239–257.

Levy, B.H. (2011) 'Bernard-Henri Lévy Defends Accused IMF Director' *The Daily Beast* May 15 2011. http://www.thedailybeast.com/articles/2011/05/16/bernard-henri-lvy-the-dominique-strauss-kahn-i-know.html Accessed 24 February 2014.

List and Pettit (2011) *Group Agency: The Possibility, Design, and Status of Corporate Agents*. Cambridge, UK: Cambridge University Press.

Locke, J. (1975) *An Essay Concerning Human Understanding*. Edited by P.H. Nidditch. Oxford, UK: Oxford University Press.

Luban, D. (2012) 'War as Punishment' *Philosophy and Public Affairs* 39 pp. 299–330.

Luban, D. (2007) 'Beyond Moral Minimalism' *Ethics and International Affairs* 20 pp. 353–360.

May, L. (2007) *War Crimes and Just War*. Cambridge, UK: Cambridge University Press.

May, L. (2008) *Aggression and Crimes against Peace*. Cambridge, UK: Cambridge University Press.

McMahan, J. (2009) *Killing in War*. Oxford, UK: Oxford University Press.

Matravers, Matt(ed.) (1999) *Punishment and Political Theory*. Oxford, UK: Hart Publishing.

Meckled-Garcia, S. (2008) 'How to Think About the Problem of Non-State Actors and Human Rights'. *Proceedings of the XXII World Congress of Philosophy* 11 pp. 41–60.

Metz, T. (2000) 'Censure Theory and Intuitions About Punishment' *Law and Philosophy* 19 pp. 491–512.

Metz, (2007) 'How to Reconcile Liberal Politics with Retributive Punishment' *Oxford Journal of Legal Studies* 27 pp. 683–705.

Michael, M.A. (1992) 'Utilitarianism and Retributivism: What's the Difference' *American Philosophical Quarterly* 29 pp. 173–182.

Morris, M. (2007) *An Introduction to the Philosophy of Language*. Cambridge, UK: Cambridge University Press.

Narayan, U. (1993) 'Appropriate Responses and Preventive Benefits: Justifying Censure and Hard Treatment in Legal Punishment' *Oxford Journal of Legal Studies* 13 pp. 166–182.

Nozick, R. (1981) *Philosophical Explanations*. Cambridge, MA: Harvard University Press.

Nussbaum, M. (1996) *The Therapy of Desire*. Princeton, NJ: Princeton University Press.

Nussbaum, M. (2001) *Upheavals of Thought.* Cambridge, UK: Cambridge University Press.

O'Neill, O. (1989) *Constructions of Reason.* Cambridge, UK: Cambridge University Press.

Pasternak, A. (2013) 'Limiting States' Corporate Responsibility' *Journal of Political Philosophy* 21(4): pp. 361–381.

Pasternak, A. (2011) 'The Distributive Effect of Collective Punishments' in *Accountability for Collective Wrongdoing.* Edited by Isaacs, T. and Vernon, R. Cambridge, UK: Cambridge University Press.

Pettit, P. (2007) 'Responsibility Incorporated' *Ethics* 117 pp. 171–201.

Primoratz, I. (1989) 'Punishment as Language' *Philosophy* 64 pp. 187– 205.

Radzik, L. (2009) *Making Amends.* Oxford, UK: Oxford University Press.

Raz, J. (1970) *The Concept of Legal System. An Introduction to the Theory of the Legal System.* Oxford, UK: Clarendon Press.

Raz, J. (1979) 'Kelsen's Theory of the Basic Norm' in *The Authority of Law. Essays on Law and Morality* pp. 122–45.

Raz, J. (1986) *The Morality of Freedom.* Oxford UK: Oxford University Press.

Roberts, R. (1999) 'Review: Emotions as Judgments' *Philosophy and Phenomenological Research* 59 pp. 793–8.

Rodogno, R. (2009) 'Shame, Guilt, and Punishment' . *Law and Philosophy* 28 pp. 429–464.

Sayre-McCord, G. (2001) 'Criminal Justice and Legal Reparations as an Alternative to Punishment' *Philosophical Issues* pp. 502– 529.

Searle, J. (1969) *Speech Acts.* Cambridge, UK: Cambridge University Press.

Skillen, Anthony (1980) 'How to Say Things With Walls' *Philosophy* 55 1980 pp. 509–23.

Sreenivasan, G. (2002) 'Errors about Errors: Virtue Theory and Trait Attribution' *Mind* 111 pp. 47–68.

Stephen, J.F. (1967) *Liberty, Equality, Fraternity.* Cambridge, UK: Cambridge University Press.

Stilz, A. (2011) 'Collective Responsibility and the State' *Journal of Political Philosophy* 19 pp. 190–208.

Tadros, V. (2011) *The Ends of Harm: The Moral Foundations of Criminal Law.* Oxford, UK: Oxford University Press.

Tadros, V. (2007). *Criminal Responsibility.* Oxford, UK: Oxford University Press.

Tasioulas, J. (2006) 'Punishment and Repentance' *Philosophy* 81 pp. 279–322.

Vinx, L. (2007) *Hans Kelsen's Pure Theory of Law: Legality and Legitimacy.* Oxford, UK: Oxford University Press.

Von Hirsch, Andrew. (1999) 'Punishment, Penance and the State' pp. 69–82 in Matravers 1999.

Von Hirsch, A. (1993) *Censure and Sanctions.* Oxford, UK: Oxford University Press.

Wells, C. (2001) *Corporations and Criminal Responsibility.* Cambridge, UK: Cambridge University Press.

Wendt, A. (2004) 'The State as Person in International Relations' *Review of International Studies* 30(2): pp. 289–316.

Wilkins, B. (2001) 'Whose Trials? Whose Reconciliation' in *War Crimes and Collective Responsibility: A Reader* .Edited by Aleksandr Jokic pp. 85–96. Malden MA: Blackwell.

Willsher, K. and Rushe D. (2011) 'Dominique Strauss-Kahn Will Fly Home to a France Divided Over His Reputation.' *The Guardian*, August 24, 2011 http://www.theguardian.com/world/2011/aug/24/dominique-strauss-kahn-france-divided Accessed 24 February 2014.

Wittgenstein, L. (1949) *Philosophical Investigations*. Oxford, UK: Blackwell.

Wringe, B. (2015) 'The Contents of Perception and the Contents of Emotion' *Noûs* 48 pp. 275–297.

Wringe, B. (2013) 'Must Punishment Be Intended to Cause Suffering?' *Ethical Theory and Moral Practice* 16 pp. 863–877.

Wringe, B. (2012). 'Collective Agents and Communicative Theories of Punishment' *Journal of Social Philosophy* 43 pp. 436–456.

Wringe, B. (2010) 'War Crimes and Expressive Theories of Punishment: Communication or Denunciation' *Res Publica* 16 pp. 119–33.

Wringe, B. (2006) 'Why Punish War Crimes: Victor's Justice and an Expressive Justification of Punishment' *Law and Philosophy* 25 pp. 159–191.

Zimmerman, M. (2011) *The Immorality of Punishment*. Buffalo, NY: Broadview Press.

Index

Printed and bound by CPI Group (UK) Ltd, Croydon, CR0 4YY